Elementary Structures
Reconsidered

Elementary Structures Reconsidered

Lévi-Strauss on Kinship

Francis Korn

UNIVERSITY OF CALIFORNIA PRESS

Berkeley and Los Angeles

University of California Press
Berkeley and Los Angeles, California

© *Francis Korn 1973*

LC NO. 73-78212

ISBN 0-520-02476-1

Printed in Great Britain

To Klaus

Contents

Contents

Figures

Tables

Preface

To publish a critique of a famous book written by a famous social anthropologist is perhaps a hardy undertaking. It is a kind of enterprise, at any rate, that calls apparently for a special justification. The present monograph has been written, nevertheless, in the conviction that to analyse what has been done, particularly if this is theoretically in vogue, can be just as useful for the understanding of social facts as to attempt something entirely novel.

I desire to thank those who helped me in maintaining this conviction during the writing of this book. In the course of the three years in which I composed the analyses presented here, I had the privilege of working under the guidance of Dr Rodney Needham at the University of Oxford. I received then not only the benefit of his extensive published work relating to my subject but his personal instruction and constant help in solving all sorts of technical, theoretical, and practical problems. This book could not possibly have been the same without his invaluable aid.

Lic. Ada Korn was so kind as to criticize my own logic, particularly in chapters 1 and 3, and encouraged me throughout. Lic. O. Cornblit, Mrs G. Lawaetz, and Mr T. Simpson kindly read and commented on chapter 1. Mrs P. Grant gave me unfailing friendly assistance which did a great deal to leave me free to write.

Dr E. R. Leach, the foremost anthropological exponent of Lévi-Strauss's views, and Dr P. G. Rivière read and commented on the manuscript.

The work was begun under the auspices of the Consejo

Nacional de Investigaciones Científicas y Técnicas (Argentina), which awarded me, while I was a lecturer in the methodology of social research at the National University of Buenos Aires, an external scholarship in order to pursue my researches in England.

F. K.

University of Oxford

Acknowledgements

Parts of this book have previously been published in other places. The following bodies are thanked for permission to reprint.

The American Anthropological Association, in respect of 'The Logic of some Concepts in Lévi-Strauss', *American Anthropologist*, **71** (1969): 70-1. The Koninklijk Instituut voor Taal-, Land- en Volkenkunde: 'The Analysis of the Term "Model" in some of Lévi-Strauss's Works', *Bijdragen tot de Taal-, Land- en Volkenkunde*, **125** (1969): 1-11; 'Terminology and "Structure": The Dieri Case', *Bijdragen tot de Taal-, Land- en Volkenkunde*, **127** (1971): 39-81. Tavistock Publications Limited and the Association of Social Anthropologists of the Commonwealth: 'A Question of Preferences: The Iatmül Case', in Rodney Needham, ed., *Rethinking Kinship and Marriage*, ASA Monographs 11 (London: Tavistock Publications, 1971), chapter 5 (pp. 99-132). The Royal Anthropological Institute of Great Britain and Ireland: 'Permutation Models and Prescriptive Systems: The Tarau Case' (in collaboration with Rodney Needham), *Man*, n.s., **5** (1970): 393-420.

The diagram on p. 91 (*Figure 21*) is reprinted from *Naven* (second edition) by Gregory Bateson, with the permission of the publishers, Stanford University Press. © 1958 by the Board of Trustees of the Leland Stanford Junior University.

Introduction

Les Structures élémentaires de la parenté, by Claude Lévi-Strauss, has acquired the stature of a classic in social anthropology. In the present monograph I wish to examine its scientific claims to this reputation.

Lévi-Strauss's work is considered a remarkable feat of analysis not only by social anthropologists, but also by a surprising number of writers in other fields. To cite the opinion of one of the most prominent modern psychologists, for Piaget the anthropological structuralism of Lévi-Strauss 'presents an exemplary character and constitutes the most striking model – neither functional nor genetic nor historical, but deductive – that has been employed in an empirical human science' (Piaget 1968: 90). For Boudon, similarly, Lévi-Strauss's treatment of marriage rules constitutes an 'exact', 'general', 'falsifiable' theory (1968: 203), and the 'scientific importance' of Lévi-Strauss's 'discoveries' in anthropology needs no further demonstration (1968: 10).

For Lévi-Strauss himself, *Les Structures élémentaires de la parenté* is 'an introduction to a general theory of kinship systems'. It is presented as an example in method, and indeed as the last word as far as the explanation of kinship systems is concerned: 'even if some aspect of the problem treated in the work were developed no new idea would need to be introduced' (Lévi-Strauss 1949: xi).[1]

---

[1] Page references to Lévi-Strauss's monograph are to the original French edition of 1949, or to the second French edition of 1967 when referring to the preface to this edition. The passages cited may readily be located in the English edition (1969) by means of the page-concordance (Korn and Needham 1969).

B

I

Les Structures élémentaires de la parenté was first published in 1949. The book constituted, according to Lévi-Strauss, a stage in his effort to produce 'a sort of inventory of mental constraints, an attempt to reduce the arbitrary to an order, to discover a necessity immanent in an illusion of liberty'. He chose kinship, he later explained, because it was a domain which might seem at first to be characterized by 'its incoherent and contingent character', and he tried to demonstrate that it was possible to reduce this domain to a 'very small number of significant propositions' (1963a: 630).

For Lévi-Strauss, 'kinship and its related notions are at the same time prior and exterior to the biological relations to which increasingly we tend to reduce them'. Kinship relations 'offer immediately to the mind a framework of logical classification; this framework, once it is conceived, is used in order to situate, by reference to these pre-established categories, individuals with whom anyone happens to be, or not to be, empirically related' (1955: 106). He is against the classification of kinship terminologies into 'descriptive' and 'classificatory' systems; 'descriptive' being the term applied to systems in which the terms designate particular relations between an individual and his parents, 'classificatory' those systems that group certain types of relatives and others, very distant or simply theoretical, in large classes. For him, 'every kinship system is at the same time descriptive and classificatory' (1955: 106).

In these views, Lévi-Strauss follows a long tradition starting perhaps with Durkheim by the end of the nineteenth century.

Durkheim criticized Kohler's *Zur Urgeschichte der Ehe* in 1897, because it implied that '[kinship] nomenclatures express links of blood' (1897: 313). He explained that if a term, in certain society, is applied to designate the actual mother, but also a series of other women, this is not because all these women are thought of as being in the same relationship of consanguinity towards the person who applies the term. It is because all those women belong to the same group, the group where the father had married, and the term thus explains the particular relationship of an individual towards the whole group designated by that term. Consanguinity is therefore a very different thing from kinship (*parenté*). 'Consanguinity is only the sufficient condition of kinship'; kinship is essentially a series of juridical and moral obligations, and these obligations are neither regulated nor classified as consanguineal relationships (1897: 316).

Lang, also, saw quite clearly that 'our ideas of sister, brother, father, mother, and so on, have nothing to do . . . with the native terms which include, indeed, but do not denote these relationships as understood by us' (1903: 101).

Lévi-Strauss's position coincides also with Kroeber's and Hocart's. Kroeber, when discussing the fallacious differentiation between 'classificatory' and 'descriptive' terms (1909), and Hocart, when talking about the 'disastrous' effects of the theory of the kinship 'extensions' (1937), both tried to establish the principles upon which relationship terminologies are built. Hocart shows that the Fijians do not need to think in terms of 'family trees' in order to classify a person. All they need, he says, is to place that person according to line ['side'] and generation. He proposes, then, that the specification of a native term should be done by reference to the principles involved in the classificatory system, and not by genealogy.

It is clear, therefore, from this position, that relationship terms denote social categories and not 'degrees' of kinship. The kind of status that a set of relationship terms denotes is peculiar to the society in which it is applied (cf. Needham 1960d). The comparability of a set of relationship terms with another can only be seen by reference to the classificatory principles involved in them.

To follow this position consistently one should think of relationship terms as social categories. In this respect, Lévi-Strauss's use of the term 'degree' throughout *Les Structures élémentaires de la parenté* introduces some confusion. He talks about 'prohibited degrees' when referring to the category of people that an individual is not allowed to marry (cf. 1949: 137, 367, 370; 1965: 17), and he actually identifies the concept of 'degree' with that of 'relationship' in paragraphs such as this: 'la notion du degré de parenté, c'est-à-dire la notion du rapport' (1949: 549). On the other hand, in a paragraph such as 'the ancient Chinese conceived of kinship not as a series of *degrees* but as a hierarchy of *categories*' (1949: 388), one is bound to think that the other systems he analyses or mentions are composed of 'a series of degrees'.

II

Whether kinship systems are composed of 'degrees' or 'categories', Lévi-Strauss's main idea is that they are always the expression of some sort of exchange between groups, which is, therefore, the origin of the different rules of marriage. In this, Lévi-Strauss follows Mauss's idea that exogamy is an exchange of women between clans (1920). For Lévi-Strauss,

> Exchange – and consequently the rule of exogamy which expresses it – has in itself a social value. It provides the means of binding men together, and of superimposing upon the natural links of kinship the henceforth artificial links . . . of alliance governed by rule (1949: 595).

The exchange appears to us under different forms, says Lévi-Strauss. It can be 'direct' or 'indirect', 'continuous' or 'discontinuous'; it sometimes appears as a cash or short-term transaction and at other times as a long-term transaction; sometimes it is 'explicit' and sometimes 'implicit'; at some times 'closed' and at others 'open'; at some times it is 'concrete' and at others it is 'symbolic'. But always it is 'the fundamental and common basis of all modalities of the institution of marriage' (1949: 592-3).

From all these dichotomies that characterize 'exchange', Lévi-Strauss uses 'closed/open' as the criterion to distinguish between the two main types of kinship structure. The exchange is *closed* 'when marriage must satisfy a special rule of alliance between marriage classes or a special rule of observance of preferential degrees', and it is *open* 'when the rule of exogamy is merely a collection of negative stipulations, which, beyond the prohibited degrees leaves a free choice' (1949: 592). From the preface to the first edition of the book under consideration, it is clear that 'elementary structures' are based on 'closed exchange', and Lévi-Strauss's definition of these structures is based on the formal character of their terminologies: 'the nomenclature permits the immediate determination of the circle of kin and that of affines'. Elementary structures, then, 'prescribe marriage with a certain type of relative . . . while defining all members of the society as relatives, divide them into two categories, viz., possible spouses and prohibited spouses' (1949: ix).

'Complex structures' do not possess this kind of terminology;

they are based on 'open exchange', and thus do not involve a positive determination of the spouse. But they 'can be explained as the result of the development or combination of elementary structures' (1949: 576).

III

Although the idea that all kinship systems express 'exchange', and the inference that all of them derive from 'closed' systems of exchange, are both controversial, the attempt to examine and define all the 'closed' systems of social classification is in itself interesting.

There is in social anthropology another long tradition that differentiates 'closed' or 'prescriptive' systems, involving a positive determination of the spouse, from 'non-prescriptive' systems (Fison, Howitt, Kroeber, Hodson, Lowie, the Leiden school). Lévi-Strauss's intention when writing *Les Structures élémentaires de la parenté* seemed to be to continue this tradition. It was thus understood by Needham, among others, who reinforced this idea by assimilating Lévi-Strauss's 'elementary structures' to 'prescriptive systems' (Needham 1962b; cf. Josselin de Jong 1952). The line of demarcation between prescriptive and non-prescriptive systems was traced by Needham, following Lévi-Strauss's own definition of 'elementary' and 'complex' structures, by reference to the formal traits of their relationship terminologies. This interpretation of Lévi-Strauss's definitions not only conferred an internal logic on his typology, but it also separated the notions of 'prescription' and 'preference' as analytically different. 'Prescription' referred to the positive determination of the spouse which articulated a prescriptive terminology; 'preference' did not refer to a particular type of terminology defining a system. In fact, 'preference' refers to a trait definable in any possible system whether 'elementary' or 'complex'. It refers either to explicit rules of marriage with a certain category of people or to the actual higher frequency of marriage to a certain category of spouse. In neither case is it definable by a formal trait of the system, and as it can be discerned in any system it does not provide the same sort of typological criterion that 'elementary/complex' was meant to supply. On the other hand, in a prescriptive system the 'preferred' category of spouse, defined either by an explicit rule or by statistical frequency, can coincide or not with the category prescribed by the terminology.

Thus Lévi-Strauss's use of both terms when referring to the prescribed category of spouse was certainly unfortunate. But if 'preferred' was translated as 'prescribed' whenever Lévi-Strauss refers to the prescribed category, the typology he offered was still coherent.

But for Lévi-Strauss the use of 'prescription' and 'preference' as synonyms is far from unfortunate. Both terms refer, as he affirms in 1965 and reaffirms in 1967 in the preface to the second edition of his book, to the same reality inasmuch as they refer to the models that represent this reality. 'Even a preferential system is prescriptive at the level of the model, while even a prescriptive system cannot but be preferential at the level of the reality.' His book, on the other hand, is 'concerned exclusively with models and not with empirical realities' (1967: 58 n. 20).

IV

The idea of the present monograph arose as the result of the effort to understand Lévi-Strauss's propositions in the light of his own reappraisal of 'elementary structures' since 1965. The main reason for writing it was to see whether or not Lévi-Strauss's proposals about elementary structures deserved to be included in the study of the particular kind of ideological systems represented by prescriptive terminologies.

While writing this monograph, and in response to the published articles that constitute preliminary versions of some of the chapters included here, I have encountered two kinds of objection that I should like now to answer. The first kind questions the usefulness of criticizing an author, particularly when one considers that his work is not an example to be followed. But if one pays critical attention to the writings of an author, it is because one is concerned with the subject treated by that author. If, moreover, one disagrees with views which are almost universally praised as being of outstanding theoretical importance, then a critique becomes a duty. In any case, the present monograph is by no means only a critique; its argument rests centrally upon a series of original analyses (cf. chapters 2, 4, 5, 6). There is in this respect an international and increasing trend towards the publication of very general assessments of Lévi-Strauss's theories, taking his empirical examples at their face value. The task seems to be, on the contrary, and as I hope I show here, to test Lévi-Strauss's assertions and propositions by intensive re-analysis.

The other class of objections expresses in various ways the defence of Lévi-Strauss made by Mary Douglas: 'I do not think it is fair to such an ebullient writer to take him literally' (1967: 50). The richness of his thought is held to lie in the very ambiguity of his style. Now, if Lévi-Strauss's intention were to write poetry, this view might have force; but his express intention was to propound a general theory of kinship systems. If, in this case, the final product of his thought is ambiguous – and Leach even finds that 'some passages of Lévi-Strauss when translated into English seem almost meaningless' (1967b: xvi-xvii) – how can anybody be sure of grasping correctly the ideas that he wishes to communicate?

If it were further argued in Lévi-Strauss's favour that to bring together the ideas on kinship expressed by Durkheim, Mauss, Kroeber, Hocart, Lowie, and others, in a solidary compendium on kinship systems, is in itself valuable, I should agree. But the value of the product of this effort, and the value of the 'small number of significant propositions' that Lévi-Strauss claims to have achieved, still remains to be determined. It also remains to be considered whether or not in the field of so-called kinship systems any 'new idea' can be introduced.

Chapter One
Incest Taboo: a Bridge

I

Les Structures élémentaires de la parenté is intended to be an introduction to a general theory of kinship systems (Lévi-Strauss 1949: xi), and it starts with the explanation of a universal phenomenon: the prohibition of incest. The first chapters of the book are devoted to the consideration of this problem and are reprinted without modifications in the second edition of the book (1967). In the preface to this second edition Lévi-Strauss states, however, that 'many new facts and the development of my own thought mean that nowadays I would no longer express myself in the same way', although he still believes that 'the prohibition of incest is to be explained entirely in terms of sociological causes' (1967: xv).

The reason why we shall consider here Lévi-Strauss's appraisal of the incest taboo as he expounded it in 1949 is that, although he says he would not express himself in the same way nowadays, he does not propose an alternative solution. Moreover, his consideration of the incest prohibitions still remains as the theoretical counterpart of his definition of 'elementary structures'. Even though it is possible to consider the validity and applicability of the concept of elementary structures quite independently from Lévi-Strauss's conception of the incest prohibitions, the ultimate reason for the very existence of elementary structures is referred by Lévi-Strauss to the analytically preliminary existence of the incest prohibitions.

The same kind of considerations apply to the analysis of the concepts of 'nature' and 'culture', as used by Lévi-Strauss in 1949. He states in the preface to the second edition of his book that his proposal is 'to trace the line of demarcation between the two orders guided by the presence or absence of articulated speech', although he would again express himself in this respect more in accordance with the new discoveries in this field (1967: xvi). As a matter of fact, when considering these concepts in *Les Structures élémentaires*, he does not trace the line of demarcation guided by the presence or absence of articulated speech but, rather, by the presence absence or of the incest prohibitions themselves. The concepts of nature and culture are, on the other hand, related to the incest prohibitions by Lévi-Strauss's own definition, and we shall try to analyse not their relevance as sociological concepts but the logic of their relationship with the incest prohibitions as established by Lévi-Strauss.

II

The explanation of the incest prohibitions consists, according to Lévi-Strauss, in discovering 'what profound and omnipresent causes account for the regulation of the relationships between the sexes in every society and age' (1949: 29).

He criticizes the older theoreticians (Havelock Ellis, Westermarck, Morgan, Frazer, Durkheim) who have dealt with the problem, because they explained it (1) by natural causes, or (2) exclusively as a cultural phenomenon, or, even when taking into account the double character – natural and cultural – of the phenomenon, (3) by proposing an extrinsic connection between them.

For Lévi-Strauss, the prohibition of incest 'is in origin neither purely cultural nor purely natural', although it belongs to both domains; he suggests it might be the source of facts where the bridge between Nature and Culture ought to be studied. It is not possible to distinguish by any experimental research, he explains, what is Nature and what is Culture in human behaviour. No 'analyse réelle' can provide an explanation of that bridge. Therefore, only a phenomenon such as the incest prohibitions possessing the characteristics of both domains, i.e. being at the same time universal and governed by rules, offers a suitable point of departure.

But Lévi-Strauss does not intend only a characterization of the 'incest taboo', he also tries to explain why it occurs, the 'profound and omnipresent cause' for its existence. It exists, Lévi-Strauss explains, because Culture always provides a rule whenever the human group is confronted with a scarce or random distributed value (cf. p. 41). In this case, women are the scarce value, and the incest taboo is the device to maximize it.

III

Let us start with the analysis of Lévi-Strauss's characterization of the incest taboo as a 'bridge' between Nature and Culture. On page 35 of *Les Structures élémentaires*, he says:

> even if the incest prohibition has its roots in nature it is only in the way it affects us as a social rule that it can be fully grasped.

But the fact is not only that it is a phenomenon that has its roots in Nature, and that it has to be apprehended as Culture; it is the domain where:

> there only, but there finally culture can and must, under pain of not existing, firmly declare 'Me first,' and tell Nature, 'You go no further' (1949: 38).

The incest taboo is, therefore, the introduction of 'Culture' into human life. Before it, 'culture is still non-existent; with it, nature's sovereignty over man is ended' (p. 31).

What are the definitions of the three terms, namely 'Culture', 'Nature', and 'incest prohibitions', involved in this reasoning? In the first three chapters of *Les Structures élémentaires*, the connotations of 'Nature' and 'Culture' are the following:

Nature is the domain of:	*Culture* is the domain of:
universality (p. 9)	particularity (p. 9)
lack of rules (p. 9)	rules (p. 9)
spontaneity (p. 12)	non-spontaneity (p. 12)
repetitive processes (p. 37)	cumulative processes (p. 37)
biological heredity (p. 37)	alliance (p. 38)

Whence he derives:

   (i) the prohibition of incest is universal;
  (ii) the prohibition of incest is a rule;
 (iii) therefore, it belongs to both domains.

In Lévi-Strauss's own words:

> This rule [the prohibition of incest] is at once social, in that
> it is a rule, and pre-social, in its universality and the type of
> relationships upon which it imposes a norm (1949: 13).

Let us examine the consistency of these definitions. The particular
concept that Lévi-Strauss is going to explain is defined by
reference to two sets, the defining characteristics of which are
pairs of opposites. The set of elements labelled as 'incest prohibitions', i.e. the rules concerning sexual relations in a group,
share two defining characteristics of the set Nature, namely,
universality and the sort of relations to which they refer, and all
the characteristics of the set Culture. In this sense, one would
say that, in fact, incest prohibitions do not belong to either of the
referential sets. 'Incest prohibitions' do not belong to Nature
because they possess only two of the defining characteristics of
this set; and they do not belong to Culture either, because while
possessing all the defining characteristics of this set, they also
possess two characteristics of the opposite set. Lévi-Strauss is
aware of this problem when he says, for instance, that the incest
taboo 'is neither purely cultural, nor purely natural' (1949: 30).

IV

It seems at this point that there are some problems here concerning
the demarcation of the sets or the application of the defining
criteria, and that these are responsible for the conceptualization
of something as belonging and not belonging to each of the opposite
sets as defined. The problem becomes more evident if one thinks
of any other possible rule. If a rule concerning incest prohibitions
belongs to Nature because of 'the type of relationships upon which
it imposes a norm', we can consider other examples in which
the connection with Nature in this sense is also obvious, thus,
rules concerning 'alimentation' or 'cooking'. They would be
considered by Lévi-Strauss as being part of Nature because of
the kind of needs they satisfy and because they would doubtless
be 'universal', but they would be also 'particular' and therefore
part of Culture as well.

In general, any rule whatsoever can be thought of as related
to 'biology' or 'basic needs' in some way. In this sense, all rules

are bound to fall within the province of Nature as well as being part of Culture because of the very fact that they are rules. Any rule can be included in a larger class defined by the sort of 'needs' it satisfies, and as such it would be considered 'universal' and as belonging to Nature, because it would then constitute 'a general condition of Culture' (Lévi-Strauss 1949: 30).

V

If the analysis of human behaviour is made by reference to Nature and Culture as opposite concepts, it seems that these concepts ought to permit a clear categorization of any fact under analysis. In other words, one of the inherent characteristics of any sort of typology or opposition used in any kind of analysis is that the opposite concepts or types have to be mutually exclusive. If they are not, this does not reveal an anomalous characteristic in the phenomenon under study but merely a defect in the typology proposed.

In the case of Lévi-Strauss's use of the concepts of Nature and Culture, the defect comes mainly from the application of the first pair of opposites listed for them, namely, universality and particularity. The fact that there are different cultural answers to a unique universal 'need' does not make these different answers 'universal': what remains universal is the 'need'. If the answers are different for each society, they are particular. The fact that in any known society there exists a certain regulation of sexual relations is no different, in a sense, from the fact that any society possesses a certain kind of political organization or a special type of economic system. But the fact that political institutions or economic systems can be defined for any known society does not lead us to consider these institutions as a part of Nature. The large variety of institutions that can be labelled as 'political' are obviously not universal. The human 'needs' to which these institutions respond are probably universal, but not the institutions themselves. And even this last phrase is controversial, because different institutions that can be categorized under the same label, i.e. 'political', 'economic', etc., can respond to different 'needs' and can therefore have very different meanings.

The case of the incest prohibitions is no different. The reasons why they do exist have to be sought in each particular case. In this sense, or even following Lévi-Strauss's own argument, the references to 'Nature' and 'Culture' when explaining the incest prohibitions do not throw any light on the problem. Moreover, it seems completely out of the question that they could do so.

VI

Apart from the definition of the incest prohibitions by reference to 'Nature' and 'Culture', the universal reason to which these rules respond, according to Lévi-Strauss, still remains to be analysed.

If the 'incest taboo' constitutes a rule, it ought to be an institutionalized deviation from random behaviour in a particular sphere of action. The sphere of action involved is sexual relations among certain social categories, and the question is to discover why in this sphere behaviour deviates from the random at all.

For Lévi-Strauss, these prohibitions have a functional value, namely to 'freeze' women within the family 'so that their distribution, or the competition for them, is within the group, and under group and not private control' (Lévi-Strauss 1949: 55).

The same idea is developed by White in a paper published in 1948. For him, the so-called 'incest taboo' should properly be considered as a form of social organization where the units involved are 'sociological rather than biological relationships' (1948: 418). Incest prohibitions and exogamy are explained in terms of cooperation (which can only take place when the evolution of articulated speech makes communication possible) and alliances. The prohibition of marriage with certain categories of people is explained, following Tylor's argument, by the imperative of 'marrying out or being killed out', as the basis of alliances between groups, the groups themselves having been formed previously because of the advantages of human cooperation.

Lévi-Strauss's own explanation does not differ very much from White's, and can be summarized as follows:

1 [Men live in groups];
2 When something is scarce (or stochastically distributed) and yet necessary for the biological continuance of a group, it becomes an 'economic good';
3 In order to 'maximize' that economic good, a group creates and transmits 'rules' about it. That is, it conceptualizes that

good as an economic good and establishes some sort of patterned behaviour in order to distribute it;

4 Women, in primitive societies, constitute an economic good because they are stochastically distributed and necessary for reproduction;

5 Some kind of organization (set of rules) is, therefore, necessary for the distribution of women;

6 The incest prohibitions are the first necessary step for such an organization.

In Lévi-Strauss's words:

> This problem of intervention [Culture introducing prohibitions of marriage] is not raised just in this particular case. It is raised, and resolved in the affirmative, every time the group is faced with the insufficiency or the risky distribution of a valuable of fundamental importance (Lévi-Strauss 1949: 39).

VII

But, for Lévi-Strauss, if the incest prohibitions constitute some sort of organization, this is not due to the prohibitions themselves but to the fact that:

> the prohibition of incest is a rule of reciprocity. The woman whom one does not take, and whom one may not take, is for that very reason, offered up (1949: 45).

Moreover,

> every prohibition is at the same time, and under another aspect, a prescription (1949: 56).[1]

This prescription is expressed in certain kinds of kinship system, those systems 'in which the nomenclature permits the immediate determination of the circle of kin and that of affines, that is those systems which prescribe marriage with a certain type of relative' and which he calls 'elementary structures' (Lévi-Strauss 1949: ix).

This is why, some years later, Lévi-Strauss explains the sequence of the themes in *Les Structures élémentaires* as follows:

[1] This phrase does not appear in the English edition (1969: 45). The editor informs me that the omission was not made at the instruction of Professor Lévi-Strauss but is the result of a regrettable oversight at one stage in the retyping of the draft translation.

The question we asked ourselves was that of the 'meaning' of the incest prohibition . . . it was necessary, then, to establish the systematic nature of each kinship terminology and its corresponding set of marriage rules (1960: 28).

VIII

Let us analyse some questions involved in Lévi-Strauss's argument. The main idea is that the incest prohibitions constitute the basis for the distribution of women because they imply at the same time a principle of reciprocity. This principle of reciprocity is expressed, as we have seen above, in the 'kinship terminology and its corresponding set of marriage rules'. But not any kinship terminology expresses the principle of reciprocity. Only those that classify, within the social group, all the possible spouses into two categories: prohibited and prescribed. That is, only those kinship systems that can be defined as 'elementary structures'. These structures contain, according to Lévi-Strauss, a distinction between parallel cousins and cross-cousins which constitutes an 'extremely simple and efficient method for maintaining an indefinite extensible balance of matrimonial exchanges between consanguineal groups'. This distinction is, on the other hand, 'nothing else than the positive aspect of a rule of which the prohibition of incest . . . represents only the negative aspect' (Lévi-Strauss 1955: 108).

Therefore the elementary structures are the reverse of the incest prohibitions; they are the conversion of a negative rule into a set of stipulations of a different order (cf. Lévi-Strauss 1949: 56).

But, in order to demonstrate that systems which prescribe a certain social category as spouse are the reverse of incest prohibitions, one should be able to prove the connection between them independently. If prescriptive systems (elementary structures) exist because there is a 'basic principle of reciprocity' underlying the incest prohibitions, one cannot give as a proof of the existence of this principle the fact that prescriptive systems do exist.

Furthermore, there is always the question of the universality of the incest prohibitions and the comparatively rare cases of societies with prescriptive systems. If 'every prohibition is at the same time . . . a prescription', then, whenever one finds prohibitions of incest one should be able to find a prescriptive rule of marriage.

This correlation is obviously not valid, and neither therefore is the argument. But the argument seems to be invalid not only because it contains logical inconsistencies, but because it includes also an erroneous conceptualization of the relationship between 'incest' and 'marriage'.

IX

We remarked above on the convenience of searching for the reasons for the existence of prohibitions of incest in each particular case. The 'meaning' of each rule prohibiting incest could vary according to the sort of social categories it involves and the kind of society where it is expressed (cf. Needham 1971b).

But even with these considerations in mind, a rule that prohibits incest cannot be the counterpart of a rule that prescribes marriage because they refer to two different things. The former refers to sexual relations, the latter to marriage. It is true that this latter concept (marriage) does not have a consolidated meaning in the anthropological literature (cf. Rivière 1971), but whatever its uses it can never be reduced to the counterpart of incest prohibitions.

Chapter Two

Structures and Regimes

I

Quite independently of the definition of elementary structures as the 'reverse' of a negative rule, the question now is to find out what Lévi-Strauss means by the term and whether the book devoted to this concept actually constitutes 'an introduction to a general theory of kinship systems' (Lévi-Strauss 1949: x).

The consideration of *Les Structures élémentaires de la parenté* as a general theory does not come only from its author but from other social scientists as well. In a recent work on the definition of the word 'structure' as used in the social sciences, Boudon classifies Lévi-Strauss's treatment of marriage rules as an 'exact', 'falsifiable', 'general' theory. This characterization places Lévi-Strauss's work at the highest degree on Boudon's scale of 'levels of verifiability' of theories. Boudon classifies theories according to two criteria: (1) whether the criterion of falsifiability is applicable or not, and (2) whether the theory is 'general' (a single theory explaining a great number of facts) or 'partial' (a number of theories each explaining a small number of facts) (Boudon 1968: 203).

Boudon does not, however, provide in his book any reason why Lévi-Strauss's treatment of marriage rules should merit such rating. The question would be to point out which of Lévi-Strauss's propositions are falsifiable and what are the 'great number of facts' that they explain. Boudon refers instead to Bush's mathematical interpretation of Lévi-Strauss's elementary structures, to a succinct 'description' of the Kariera rules of marriage and 'marriage types', and to the axioms by which Kemeny, Snell, and Thompson formulate the basic traits of elementary structures.[1] After these

---

[1] Bush's work and Kemeny, Snell, and Thompson's formulations are analysed in chapter 7 below.

references, one still does not know what are the facts that are meant to be explained and what the propositions to be falsified.

In any case, and as we state in detail in chapter 7 below, we do not think that either Bush's formulations or Kemeny, Snell, and Thompson's axioms translate Lévi-Strauss's treatment of marriage rules or any other possible theory with an ethnographic reference. Because of this, Boudon's statements on the scientific status of Lévi-Strauss's proposals remain to be considered.

II

According to its author, *Les Structures élémentaires de la parenté* 'constitutes . . . an introduction to a general theory of kinship systems' (Lévi-Strauss 1949: x). He classifies these systems under two headings: elementary structures and complex structures. Elementary structures are defined as:

> those systems in which the nomenclature permits the immediate determination of the circle of kin and that of affines, that is, those systems which prescribe marriage with a certain type of relative (1949: ix).

Complex structures on the other hand are:

> systems which limit themselves to defining the circle of relatives and leave the determination of the spouse to other mechanisms, economic or psychological (1949: ix).

In the light of these definitions, the book seems to be concerned with a dichotomous classification of societies, the types in which are distinguished by the presence or absence of a prescriptive terminology, i.e. a terminology that establishes to which terminological category the possible spouse belongs.[2]

In this sense Lévi-Strauss proposes, at least by definition, a dichotomous nominal typology of kinship systems. He does not, then, propose a 'continuum', as he himself thinks he does and as Fox interprets the elementary–complex typology.[3] When it comes to analysing the above definitions of 'elementary' and 'complex',

---

[2] For the sake of clarity we deliberately leave aside Lévi-Strauss's use of the term 'preference' as synonymous with 'prescription' in the definitions already discussed. The problems raised by the synonymous use of the two concepts in the context of Lévi-Strauss's definitions of 'elementary' and 'complex' are specifically analysed in chapter 3 below.

[3] cf. Fox 1969.

the only criterion stipulated by Lévi-Strauss is whether or not a given society prescribes marriage with a certain type of relative. Thus, it is hard to see how Fox can assert that 'all complex systems are complex, but some are more complex than others' (Fox 1967: 222) if what matters is the presence or absence of a certain kind of prescription derived from the articulation of the relationship terminology. According to this typology, a system is to be classified either as 'elementary' or as 'complex', and the consideration of degrees is by definition excluded. Hence the characterization of Crow–Omaha systems as an 'intermediary type' (Lévi-Strauss 1967: xxxvi) is meaningless; for this necessarily implies that a possible third type can be defined in Lévi-Strauss's typology, which is inconceivable by the very nature of the criterion employed. First of all, there is no continuum involved: according to Lévi-Strauss's definition of the kinds of structure, Crow–Omaha systems are merely another case of 'complex structures' because they do not contain a prescriptive category of spouse (Lévi-Strauss 1949: ix). The fact that they imply a wide range of prohibitions and that therefore the 'choices' are fewer, does not make them any the less complex, since complex, as defined by Lévi-Strauss, means that they are non-prescriptive and not that they offer a greater or lesser choice.[4] On the other hand, Lévi-Strauss himself says:

> The Crow Indians are divided into thirteen exogamous clans. All we learn from this is that a man can regard twelve out of thirteen woman as a possible spouse. Apart from the scale, *the marriage rule is as indeterminate as in our society* (1949: 92).[5]

The degree of choice could constitute a secondary criterion distinguishing subtypes within complex structures, but it is not mentioned as such in *Les Structures élémentaires de la parenté*.

[4] We follow here Lévi-Strauss's reasoning in the preface to the second French edition of *Les Structures élémentaires de la parenté* (pp. xxiv-xxx), which is different from the ideas expressed in 1949: 576, where Crow–Omaha systems are considered as sometimes having and sometimes not having a prescriptive rule (cf. Needham 1964b: 312-13).

[5] As a matter of fact, with only these specifications to go on, we certainly cannot be sure that for a Crow man 'twelve out of thirteen women' are a 'possible spouse'. The information that the Crow Indians have thirteen exogamous clans can tell us only that a Crow looking for a wife can choose from all the women of the Crow society minus the number of women belonging to his own particular clan. But any anthropologist dealing with the Crow society would correct this information, knowing – by the very definition of the type – that at least two clans in addition to Ego's will be forbidden as sources of a wife.

Quite apart from their classification in the elementary–complex typology, there is still a prior matter to be discussed when considering Crow–Omaha 'systems'. Needham's analysis of the Gurage terminology (1969) concludes that the so-called 'Crow–Omaha' terminological traits do not amount to a distinct class of terminologies. These traits do not characterize systems other than the Crow and the Omaha themselves.

III

Going back to Boudon's views on the classification of theories, when he comes to consider the levels of verifiability of theories, the emphasis is on the object: 'We should note . . . the close correlation between the level of verification reached and the characteristics of the object studied' (Boudon 1968: 202). So what is the object of Lévi-Strauss's theory? According to Boudon, it is the study of marriage rules, and this object has a fascinating characteristic, namely: 'the rules of marriage can be analysed by reference to the rules of marriage alone' (Boudon 1968: 202).

In fact, the object is not marriage rules but elementary structures, as the very title of Lévi-Strauss's book states. There is a correlation between the two concepts, of course, but 'marriage rules' cover a wider field than 'elementary structures'. For Lévi-Strauss, the rules are only one of the elements of the structure (cf. 1949: ix). Complex structures, on the other hand, were to form the subject of a separate work (cf. 1949: x).

For Lévi-Strauss, the 'basic purpose' of *Les Structures élémentaires de la parenté* is 'to show that marriage rules, nomenclature, and the system of rights and prohibitions are indissociable aspects of one and the same reality, viz., the structure of the system under consideration' (1949: ix). Thus, the 'introduction to a general theory' that the book is meant to contain refers to the interrelation of the composite elements of those systems that can be defined as elementary structures.

Unless the structure of a system is something different from the ensemble of marriage rules, nomenclature, and rights and prohibitions, the book is meant to be concerned with a description and definition of the different types of elementary structures. None of the component elements of the structure (marriage rules, nomenclature, and rights and prohibitions) is considered by Lévi-Strauss independently from the others. The description of their inter-relation in each type of elementary structure would not in itself be explanatory, therefore, unless each particular inter-relationship defining each particular type of elementary structure were related to something else, independent from the structure. Only this last kind of relationship between types of structure and an independent variable can be considered an explanatory proposition concerning the former. We shall consider the existence of this sort of proposition contained in Lévi-Strauss's book in the following section.

With respect to the concept of 'structure' as used in *Les Structures élémentaires de la parenté*, there is no consistent meaning of the term throughout the book. 'Structure' is assimilated by Lévi-Strauss to 'regulating principle', or to the Gestalt concept of 'whole' (cf. 1949: 129), or alternatively to the division of societies into actual institutions such as moieties, sections, and subsections (cf. 1949: 274-5).

IV

In the book under consideration there is no explanatory proposition to account for the existence of elementary structures, except for the fallacious relation between a 'basic principle of reciprocity' and these structures, which we have already analysed in chapter 1 above. The general principle of exchange that, according to Lévi-Strauss, underlies any kinship system (cf. Lévi-Strauss 1949: 592-3), as it is common to all of them, does not 'explain' any particular type. The different types of exchange do not 'explain' any particular kind of elementary structure, because these structures are defined by means of the modes of exchange they imply.

But there is in *Les Structures élémentaires de la parenté* at least one explanatory proposition relating different types of exchange, i.e. different subtypes of elementary structures, and something else. This is the relationship postulated by Lévi-Strauss between types of exchange and 'regimes', as we shall see below.

There are three possible elementary structures, says Lévi-Strauss, and they are constructed by means of two forms of exchange (1949: 611). These two forms of exchange are 'restricted' exchange and 'generalized' exchange. 'Exchange' refers to the

22 *Elementary Structures Reconsidered*

'exchange of women' among a number of units. Systems of restricted exchange are those 'which effectively or functionally divide the group into a certain number of pairs of exchange units so that, for any pair X–Y there is a reciprocal exchange relationship. In other words, where an X man marries a Y woman, a Y man must always be able to marry an X woman' (1949: 189). The 'formula' of a system of 'restricted' exchange is therefore the representation of a symmetric relationship: A⇄B. Cross-cousin marriage is the 'privileged case' (1949: 186), and Australia the 'privileged area' of this type of exchange (1949: 190). In Australia it is possible to find 'the different systems of restricted exchange,

Figure 1 Restricted exchange: moiety system

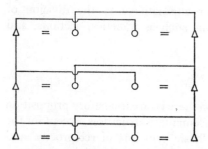

viz., dual organization, the four-section system, and the eight-subsection system' (1949: 190). The simplest form of a system of 'restricted' exchange is a 'moiety' system, the representation of which is as in *Figure 1*. This system merely requires the differentiation between parallel and cross-cousins, regardless of whether the latter are patrilateral or matrilateral. Cross-cousins of both sides are, in principle, included in the prescribed category.

The second type of exchange, generalized, differs from restricted exchange by the way in which 'reciprocity' takes place and by the number of units involved in a single transaction of exchange. In the 'generalized' or 'indirect' form, exchange takes place among more than two units. Women are transferred from one unit to another, i.e. A→B→C→(A). For this kind of exchange a further differentiation between patrilateral and matrilateral cross-cousins is required. If the system is based on MBD marriage, the 'exchange' is 'continuous' as is represented in *Figure 2*. If, instead, the system

Figure 2 MBD marriage: continuous exchange

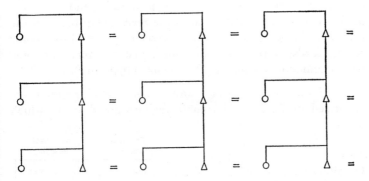

is based on FZD marriage, the 'exchange' is 'discontinuous', i.e. there are two different cycles (cf. *Figure 3*).

Figure 3 FZD marriage: discontinuous exchange

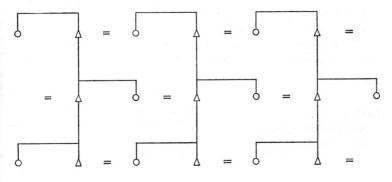

V

Thus Lévi-Strauss distinguishes three types of elementary structures that are defined by (i) the type of exchange, i.e. restricted or generalized; and by (ii) the 'continuous' or 'discontinuous' character of the exchange.

The systems categorized by the two kinds of exchange, i.e. restricted and generalized, are related by Lévi-Strauss to another variable, namely, the relationship between the rule of residence and the rule of descent, a relationship that he calls 'regime'. In his own words, the relationship between 'structures' and 'regimes' is as follows:

The whole imposing apparatus of prescriptions and prohibitions could be reconstructed *a priori* from one question and one alone: in the society concerned, what is the relationship between the rule of residence and the rule of descent? Every disharmonic regime leads to restricted exchange, just as every harmonic regime announces generalized exchange (1949: 612).

His definitions of 'harmonic' and 'disharmonic' regimes are summarized in *Table 1*. Harmonic regimes are those in which

	Patrilineal descent	Matrilineal descent
Patrilocal residence	Harmonic	Disharmonic
Matrilocal residence	Disharmonic	Harmonic

Table 1
Definition of harmonic and disharmonic regimes

locality and descent follow the same matrilineal or patrilineal principle. Disharmonic regimes are those in which locality and descent follow opposite principles.

The relationship that Lévi-Strauss establishes between type of structure (restricted or generalized exchange) and regime (harmonic or disharmonic) is as in *Table 2*. Hence the relationship

	Harmonic regime	Disharmonic regime
Structures of restricted exchange	–	+
Structures of generalized exchange	+	–

Table 2
Relationship between regime and structure

between regime and structure is falsifiable, because it proposes an empirical relationship between two independently defined variables, namely type of structure and type of regime. Any empirical example of a system with a harmonic regime and a structure of restricted exchange, or of a system with a disharmonic regime and a structure of generalized exchange, would be a refutation of Lévi-Strauss's proposition.

VI

The trouble is that Lévi-Strauss's book itself provides the refutation. We shall examine here one of the typical examples of restricted exchange, i.e. the eight-subsection 'structure' of the Aranda system, as presented by Lévi-Strauss.

The Aranda are presented by Lévi-Strauss as one of the classical examples of 'restricted exchange' because they exchange sisters. They marry a person categorized by a term the genealogical description of which is 'second cross-cousin', that is, the people who intermarry are the children of cross-cousins. The case is important in Lévi-Strauss's argument, because it represents 'the second dichotomy of the disharmonic regime', that is, there is a distinction between first cross-cousins and second cross-cousins (1949: 272), and it makes understandable how systems of harmonic regimes (and consequently, of generalized exchange) are intermediary in function between two disharmonic regimes, namely, the Kariera and the Aranda (1949: 217). This functional series permits Lévi-Strauss to construct his 'general table' of the relationship between harmonic and disharmonic regimes (1949: 273, Figure 44).

As seems to be the rule in Australia, the Aranda are patrilocal. In this, Lévi-Strauss follows Pink, who 'was able to speak of the Northern Aranda as "landowners", among whom the "ancestral clan state" and the patrilineal line by which it is transmitted together with the ritual, play a leading part in both collective and individual life' (1949: 193).

On the question of which grouping is to be considered 'owners' of the land, Lévi-Strauss says that 'the question is not so much whether it is the horde or the clan which should be considered the real landowning group, but which of these two patrilineal groups is at the basis of the social organization' (1949: 193).

As for the rule by which an Aranda man belongs to one of the eight subsections, Lévi-Strauss says: 'in the Aranda system a man falls into the same class as his grandfather (FF) and he always finds his grandson (SS) in the same class as himself' (1949: 171).

He also says that 'in the final analysis it is the relationship of consanguinity which plays the principal role, while class membership, at least in practice, is secondary' (1949: 165). In this respect, the representation of the relationship terms in his diagram of the Aranda system (1949: 214, Figure 15) arranges them in the form of four patrilines.

So far, all the indications would point to a 'harmonic regime'

in Lévi-Strauss's terms. The Aranda certainly seem to be patrilocal, and whatever Lévi-Strauss means by 'descent' he mentions
patrilineal hordes, patrilineal clans, patrilineal determination of
membership to a subsection, and represents the system formally by
patrilines. Yet he also says that in the Aranda type 'descent and
residence are transmitted in separate lines' (1949: 270). By this, he
can only mean that 'descent' is transmitted separately from the
patrilocal residence that he recognizes, i.e. matrilineally. As we
have already seen, however, he gives no indication of any right or
membership to a group that could be conceptualized as 'descent'
and which is transmitted in this way. Even if we take into account
Leach's observation that 'Lévi-Strauss . . . confuses the notion of
descent, a legal principle governing the transmission of rights from
generation to generation, with the notion of *filiation*, the kinship
link between parent and child' (Leach 1969a: 101), the representation of this latter link in Lévi-Strauss's diagram is still patrilineal.
The only instances in which he refers to some kind of matrilineal
transmission among the Aranda are (1) his representation of an
eight-subsection system by which the child of a couple takes the
name of the mother and the residence of the father (1949: 212,
Figure 14), and (2) a paragraph in which he refers to matrilineal
moieties among the Aranda (1949: 272).

With regard to Lévi-Strauss's representation of an eight-
subsection system mentioned above, he does not refer to any
trait of the Aranda system that could correspond to the matrilineal
transmission of the 'name'. On the other hand, no such trait is
reported in the ethnographical accounts of the Aranda. With
regard to the moieties, although these were referred to as 'matrilineal' by Durkheim (1902: 109) and by Radcliffe-Brown (1931: 27),
among others, they are not in fact reported as such by the ethnographers.

VII

Spencer and Gillen, in their first account, say that among the
Aranda 'descent is counted in the male line' (1899: 68). They
reaffirm this view still in 1927, when they say: 'the child passes
into the father's moiety, but not into a section (or subsection)
to which he does not belong; that is, descent is counted in the
indirect male line' (1927: 43). According to Spencer and Gillen

also, the totemic name of an individual among the Aranda is not related to the totem name of the father or to that of the mother, although it can coincide with them in some cases. This is possible because, among the Aranda, the totemic groups are not exogamous.

Spencer and Gillen compare the descent system of the Aranda with that of the Arabana and they say that the systems are 'male in the Arunta, female in the Urabuna' (1927: 43 n. 1). When they explain how the Arabana classify a Southern Aranda in terms of their own system, Spencer and Gillen make an equivalence between the matrilineal moieties of the Arabana and the four sections of the Southern Aranda (where 'descent is counted in the indirect male line'). They do not refer to equivalences between the Arabana matrilineal moieties and the putative Aranda matrilineal moieties, because among the latter these matrilineal moieties do not exist.

Mathews, however, tried to prove in 1908 that descent among the Aranda was in fact matrilineal. By 'descent' he meant the principle by which an Aranda individual was ascribed to a section or subsection, because what he tries to demonstrate is that the interpretation of the tables presented by his informants, showing that an Aranda individual belongs to the section or subsection to which his or her father's father belongs, is wrong. Using the same tables, he claims to have demonstrated that an Aranda individual belongs to the section to which his or her mother's mother's mother's mother belonged (1908: 96). The fact that the Aranda also take the name of their father's father does not constitute for Mathews a diagnostic feature in the consideration of 'descent', because he says that 'in fact, in every tribe I know possessing female descent, all over Australia, the child takes the name of the father's father' (1908: 95). This last statement by Mathews is curious because, at the time he wrote it, the reports of Gason and Howitt about the Dieri were already known. Even though the Dieri did not have sections or subsections, they certainly were matrilineal, and the term by which they classified a person was the term by which they classified his or her mother's mother's brother, and not his or her father's father.

In any case, Mathew's conclusions about the Aranda were contested by the most authoritative and detailed ethnographic report on the Aranda, namely Strehlow's *Die Aranda- und Loritja-Stämme in Zentral-Australien* (1907-20).

Referring to the article by Mathews mentioned above, Strehlow says that Mathews, in his attempts to show that the Aranda were matrilineal, used Strehlow's own material without citing the source. With respect to Mathew's conclusions, he says that 'it cannot be too strongly stressed that R. H. Mathews groups the marriage classes of the Aranda in a quite arbitrary way in order to prove his theory' (part IV, I, 1913: 71).

According to Strehlow, both the eight classes of the Northern Aranda and the four classes of the Southern Aranda are divided into two major groups. Although Spencer and Gillen say that these two groups or moieties are not named, Strehlow reports three different sets of names for them, as used by the Aranda. They call them Alurinja, the moiety that in the Southern Aranda is divided into the Purula and the Kamara sections, and Kwatjarinja, the moiety that in the same region is divided into the Panaka and the Paltara sections.

The Aranda also apply the terms Nákarakia and Etnákarakia to these divisions. Nákarakia derives from *nuna*, we, *na*, father, and *inkaraka*, all; thus the term is translated by Strehlow as 'we the fathers and everybody', i.e. 'our whole kindred' or 'all of us'. Etnákarakia derives from *etna*, they, and *inkaraka*, all; the term is therefore translated as 'their fathers and everybody' or 'their whole kindred' or 'all of them' (Strehlow 1907-20; part IV, I: 62). On page 63, Strehlow further translates Etnákarakia as 'those people'. These two terms, Nákarakia and Etnákarakia, are not absolute designations of groups, but are relative terms which designate reciprocally own moiety and the opposite moiety (p. 62).

The third set of names by which the Aranda designate their moieties are Lakakia, which corresponds to Nákarakia and means 'our people', and Maljanuka, which corresponds with Etnákarakia and means 'my friends' (Strehlow 1907-20; part IV, I: 63).

Children belong to the class of their father's father, Strehlow says, and when a 'wrong' marriage takes place, that is, when a man marries a woman who is not his *noa* ('wife'), the child born of such a marriage is also 'ascribed to the class of his father's father (paternal grandfather)'. He then adds that 'these cases only confirm the rule that the class is transmitted in the paternal line, not in the maternal' (1907-20; part IV, I: 71).

In accordance with this, Pink, who was also among the Aranda, says: 'when "wrong" marriages do take place, the problem of descent is mechanically solved by the children invariably going into the other couple of subsections to their father, thus utterly ignoring their mother's subsection' (1936: 297).

The list of terms in Strehlow's report is reproduced in *Table 3*.[6]

Table 3

Aranda Relationship Terms

(from Strehlow 1907-20; part IV, I: 66-70)

1.	*aranga*	FF, FFeB, FFyB, FFZ, WFM, SS, SD, BSS, BSD, WZSS, WZSD
2.	*palla*	FM, FMZ, FMB, WFF, ZSS, ZSD, WBSS, WBSD, HBSS, HBSD
3.	*tjimia*	MF, MFeB, MFyB, MFZ, WMM, HMM, DS, DD, BDS, BDD, WZDS, WZDD
4.	*ebmanna*	MM, MMZ, MMB, WMF, ZDS, ZDD, WBDS, WBDD, FZSW, MBSW, DS (w.s.), DD (w.s.)
5.	*kata*	F, FB
6.	*knaia*	F (w.s.), FB (w.s.), SSS
7.	*maia*	M, MZ, FBW
8.	*wonna*	FZ, MBW
9.	*kamuna*	MB, FZH, DH, BDH, WZDH
10.	*antara*	WF, WFZ
11.	*marra*	WM, DH (w.s.), DHB (w.s.), WBSW, WBDH, ZDH, ZSW
12.	*kalja*	eB, FeBS, MeZS, MeZH
13.	*itia*	yB, FyBS, MyZS, WyZH, HyZH, yZ, FyBD, MyZD, WyBW, HyBW
14.	*kwaia*	eZ, FeBD, MeZD, WeBW, HeBW
15.	*ankalla*	FeZS, MeBS, FyZS, MyBS, FeZD, MeBD, FyZD, MeBD
16.	*noa*	W, WZ, FBSW, H, HB, FBDH (w.s.), MZDH (w.s.)
17.	*mbana*	WB, ZH, FBDH, MZSW
18.	*intanga*	HZ, eBW (w.s.), yBW (w.s.), FBSW (w.s.), MZSW (w.s.)
19.	*iliarra*	FZDH, MBDH
20.	*alirra*	S, D, BS, BD, HZS, HZD, [FFF]
21.	*amba*	ZS, ZD, WBD, HBS, HBD, HF, S (w.s.), D (w.s.), ZC (w.s.)
22.	*namara*	SW, BSW, WZSW, HF
23.	*nêrra*	SW (w.s.), ZSW (w.s.), HBSW, HM

[6] Strehlow arranges the terms by 'classes', i.e. *aranga, palla,* etc., and gives a descriptive combination of terms for each genealogical specification within each class, e.g. *aranga knara,* FFeB, *aranga larra,* FFyB, etc.

According to this table, a diagram can be drawn of the Aranda relationship terms as in *Figure 4*. In this diagram it is possible to see that the terms compose four patrilines, that they alternate by genealogical level in each line, and that they can also be arranged symmetrically.

T. G. H. Strehlow, who in 1947 talks about the 'typically Aranda patrilineal order' (1947: 71), reproduces in his book Fry's table of the relationship between subsections (Fry 1931). This

Figure 4 Aranda relationship terminology (cf. *Table 3*)

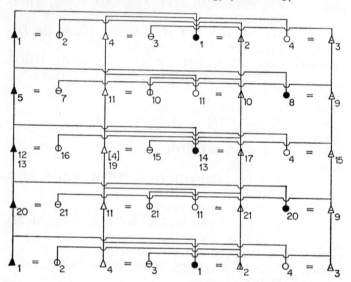

table is consistent with the data provided by Spencer and Gillen and by C. Strehlow, and we have arranged it as in *Figure 5*. From *Figures 4* and *5* it can be seen that the arrangement of the relationship term is perfectly consistent with the arrangement of subsections. In both cases, the same principles are followed. In *Figure 4* there are four patrilines arranged in two formal divisions, and in *Figure 5* there are four lines of subsections that are also patrilineally transmitted and belong to two moieties. The moieties, as we have seen, were actually patrilineal, i.e. they each contained four subsections patrilineally transmitted, and were actually named. The terms alternate according to genealogical level within the patrilines (see *Figure 4*), and the subsections are also transmitted by alternate genealogical level within the same moiety and the same line. The terms are disposed symmetrically in *Figure 4*, and the relationship between subsections, as shown in *Figure 5*, is also symmetrical.

With regard to totemic groups, all the ethnographers concur in their findings that none of the totemic groups definable for the Aranda was exogamous.

Figure 5 Relationship between subsections among the Aranda (after Fry, in Strehlow 1947: 173-4)

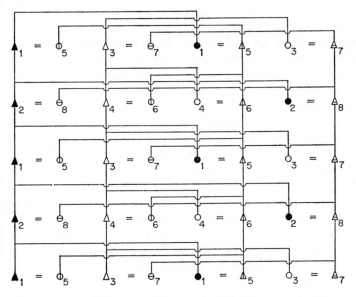

Note: 1 = Panaka   2 = Banata   3 = Knurea   4 = Paltara
      5 = Purula   6 = Kamara   7 = Nala   8 = Mbijana

C. Strehlow refers to two kinds of totem. Every individual belongs to one totem that is neither patrilineal nor matrilineal but which depends on the place where the mother first became aware of her pregnancy. Thus the children of one mother can belong to different conceptional totems (*ratapa*). At the same time, every individual also belongs to another totem (*altjirà*), which is inherited from the mother: 'thus, each individual is connected with two totems; one totem to which he belongs by birth and the second which belongs to him and which is inherited by him through his mother' (Strehlow 1907-20; part II, II: 58).

T. G. H. Strehlow does not, however, refer to totems inherited from the mother, but to the conception-site totem and to the local totemic clans that include the 'own nearest male relatives' (1947: 120). In his account, even the *tjurunga* objects and ceremonies that 'belong' to an individual, and depend on the conception-site totem, are passed, after the death of the owner, into the possession of his son or of some other male relative if the son is still too young (1947: 133).

VIII

Durkheim, basing his argument on the Spencer and Gillen report of 1899, infers the previous existence of matrilineal 'phratries' among the Aranda in order to explain the formation of the sections and subsections. His hypothesis is that they had matrilineal moieties and matrilineal exogamous totems, which, in combination with the patrilocal groups, produced the system of sections and subsections (1902: 109-11). Once the new divisions (all of them patrilineal) were established, the former matrilineal groups lost their function of regulating relationships and, as such, they disappeared.

Radcliffe-Brown in 1931 talks about matrilineal moieties among the Aranda, but in his case they seeem to be a formal inference from the composition of the relationship terminology. 'The Aranda system of eight subsections, of course, involves the existence of a pair of matrilineal moieties though they are unnamed' (Radcliffe-Brown 1931: 27).

For Lévi-Strauss, instead, the matrilineal moieties and matrilineal descent among the Aranda seem to be not an inference but a fact. The moieties are 'elements' of the system. In his own words:

> The generalized system goes beyond the Kariera system since it employs the same number of elements as the Aranda system, if not of the same nature: two moieties (patrilineal in one case, matrilineal in the other), and a four-component complex (of lines in one and local groups in the other) (Lévi-Strauss 1949: 272).

The matrilineal moieties of the Aranda are thus for Durkheim a hypothetical condition for an evolutionary explanation, for Radcliffe-Brown an inferred entity, and for Lévi-Strauss objective institutions defining 'descent', even when their existence is not reported in the ethnography.

Lévi-Strauss represents the Aranda system by the names of two French families and four French towns, 'following the double stipulation that the family name be transmitted in the maternal line, and the residential name in the paternal line' (1949: 212). The system is then said to be homologous to the following combinations:

If a man	marries a woman	the children will be
Durand of Caen	Dupont of Laon	Dupont of Caen
Durand of Laon	Dupont of Lille	Dupont of Laon
Durand of Lille	Dupont of Lyons	Dupont of Lille
Durand of Lyons	Dupont of Caen	Dupont of Lyons
Dupont of Caen	Durand of Lyons	Durand of Caen
Dupont of Laon	Durand of Caen	Durand of Laon
Dupont of Lille	Durand of Laon	Durand of Lille
Dupont of Lyons	Durand of Lille	Durand of Lyons

No matrilineal descent groups are reported in the Aranda ethnography. The only hint of a matrilineal transmission of anything among the Aranda is the inheritance of the *altjirà* totem from the mother, reported by C. Strehlow. Lévi-Strauss, however, does not so much as mention this source of evidence.[7] Yet even supposing that these hypothetical matrilineal moieties, either recognized by the Aranda or inferred by the analyst, could be established, this solitary matrilineal transmission could not be the fundamental characterization of 'descent' when all the other factors that define the status of an Aranda individual are transmitted patrilineally.

IX

Durkheim proposed the hypothesis of former matrilineal moieties in order to account for the existence of sections and subsections as far as they contained categories belonging to alternate genealogical levels. That is, he was explaining the alternation.

For Lévi-Strauss, instead, the main issue is the relationship

[7] In *La Pensée sauvage* (1962), Lévi-Strauss cites both the fourth volume of Strehlow's *Die Aranda- und Loritja-Stämme in Zentral-Australien* and T. G. H. Strehlow's *Aranda Traditions* (1947). He describes the Aranda as having 'filiation patrilinéaire', totemic affiliation not dependent on a rule of descent, non-exogamous totemic groups, and eight subsections (1962: 108). On the very next page, nevertheless, he again represents the Aranda system as composed of matrilineal moieties (1962: 109).

D

between disharmonic regimes and 'restricted exchange'. He employs Durkheim's independent variables (patrilocality and matrilinearity), but as the cause of a different consequence.

Right or wrong, Durkheim's hypothesis has a logical argument. Lévi-Strauss's hypothesis, by contrast, establishes a link between two variables which are not logically related. Apart from the fact that the Aranda system seems to refute the hypothesis, there is no demonstrated logical connection between patrilocal residence, matrilineal descent, and a symmetric rule of marriage.

In Durkheim's hypothesis symmetric exchange is a condition: the societies considered possessed, according to him, exogamous matrilineal 'phratries' and patrilocal groups. These two factors are together responsible for the separation of alternate generations into different sections or subsections. Adjacent generations within a single group belong to different matrilineal moieties, and this is the reason why they are separated into different sections. In other words, adjacent generations within a single patrilocal group belong to different moieties, but as they live together they are 'too near' to intermarry (Durkheim 1898: 19).

For Lévi-Strauss, symmetric exchange is not a condition but a result. 'Every disharmonic regime leads to restricted exchange,' he says; also, the form of exchange 'depends' on the harmonic or disharmonic character of the regime considered (1949: 612). But a disharmonic regime 'leads' (*conduit*) to restricted exchange when restricted exchange existed already, and what Lévi-Strauss is really trying to explain is the passage from one form of restricted exchange to another. This can be seen from the following quotation:

> disharmonic systems have naturally developed towards organizations with marriage classes, because, in such systems, direct exchange is the simplest and most effective process for ensuring the integration of the group (Lévi-Strauss 1949: 550).

Thus 'restricted', 'direct', or 'symmetric' exchange[8] already exists before disharmonic regimes can 'lead' to another form of restricted exchange. The kind of restricted exchange that is prior to the relationship between disharmonic regimes and another form of restricted exchange is a system with exogamous moieties.

[8] Lévi-Strauss employs these three adjectives to qualify the same kind of exchange.

'The moiety system is based solely upon descent, and the harmonic or disharmonic features of the corresponding regime are confused' (Lévi-Strauss 1949: 273). From here, the pronouncement that the form of exchange 'depends' on the harmonic or disharmonic character of the regime is difficult to follow. It is also difficult to understand how one can 'reconstruct *a priori*' the kind of exchange structure one is dealing with 'from one question and one alone: in the society concerned, what is the relationship between the rule of residence and the rule of descent' (1949: 612). How can one know beforehand when the harmonic or disharmonic features of the regime are going to be 'confused'? Or is one to think that when 'regime' cannot be defined because 'locality' and 'descent' are 'confused', one is not dealing with an 'elementary structure'? If this were so, a system with exogamous moieties and a corresponding two-line symmetric prescriptive terminology could not be classified as an elementary structure. This would certainly be an odd conclusion.

Either restricted exchange 'depends' on disharmonic regimes or it does not. If it does in some cases and does not in some others, one cannot 'reconstruct *a priori*', from the indications of the rule of residence and the rule of descent, what the mode of exchange will be.

X

To return to Boudon's characterization of Lévi-Strauss's theory, the hypothesis considered above does not explain 'a great number of facts'. What is more, it can be shown to be false. On the other hand, if by 'les règles de mariage peuvent être analysées à partir des seules règles du mariage' Boudon refers to Lévi-Strauss's 'deduction' of the rule of marriage with the matrilateral cross-cousin and the rule of marriage with the second cross-cousin from the rule of marriage with the bilateral cross-cousin, this deduction is neither supported by the facts nor reduced to a relationship between rules of marriage. Lévi-Strauss's logical derivation of the matrilateral or patrilateral cross-cousin marriage and of the second cross-cousin marriage from cross-cousin marriage, takes into account a factor other than the rules, namely harmonic and disharmonic regimes; and in any case neither the logical relation between the rules nor their relationship to another factor can be confirmed with the very facts he presents.

Chapter Three

Prescription and Preference

In 'The Future of Kinship Studies' (1965) and in the new preface to the second French edition of *Les Structures élémentaires de la parenté*,[1] Lévi-Strauss's statements about 'elementary structures' pose with new precision the problem whether his typology can still be considered a useful analytical scheme.

As we have already seen, 'elementary' and 'complex' structures were originally defined by Lévi-Strauss as follows:

> Elementary structures of kinship are those systems . . . which prescribe marriage with a certain type of relative. . . . The term 'complex structures' is reserved for systems which . . . leave the determination of the spouse to other mechanisms (1949: ix).

Even though his own definition states literally that 'elementary structure' implies prescription, Lévi-Strauss devotes the main part of the new preface to making quite clear his disagreement with Needham's (1962a) interpretation of 'elementary structures' as prescriptive systems. Lévi-Strauss insists that the rather indiscriminate use of words 'prescriptive' and 'preferential' in his book is not an unfortunately vague way of writing but has to do with a theoretical issue.

I intend to analyse here the logical consistency of Lévi-Strauss's typology by reference to the analytical criteria he employs, namely: elementary, complex; prescriptive, preferential; prohibition, choice; mechanical, statistical.

The above quotation on the definition of 'elementary' and

---

[1] The preface has also been published separately under the title 'Vingt ans après', in *Les Temps Modernes*, CCLXV, 1967: 385-406.

'complex' structures, and the subsequent line of analysis developed in the book, make it clear that the term 'elementary' denotes the existence of a positive rule concerning a certain category of individuals. Later, however, Lévi-Strauss adds:

> All systems of kinship and marriage contain an 'elementary' core which manifests itself in the incest prohibition (1965: 18).

Therefore either prescriptions or prohibitions affecting marriage with an individual of a particular social category are the 'elementary' core of a system.

'Complex structures', on the other hand, are concerned with 'choice'. This factor is introduced by the existence of various 'mechanisms' other than a prescriptive rule. Lévi-Strauss asserts that:

> all systems have a 'complex' aspect, deriving from the fact that more than one individual can usually meet the requirements of even the most prescriptive systems, thus allowing for a certain freedom of choice (1965: 18).

Therefore, the term 'complex' undoubtedly implies 'choice'. The first equations that can be established, then, are:

$$\text{prohibition} = \text{elementary} \qquad (1)$$
$$\text{choice} = \text{complex.} \qquad (2)$$

Concerning models, Lévi-Strauss states that there are:

> societies which (as even our own) have a mechanical model to determine prohibited marriages and rely on a statistical model for those which are permissible (1958: 311).

Thus the representation of prohibited and possible marriages implies a code whereby:

$$\text{prohibition} = \text{mechanical} \qquad (3)$$
$$\text{choice} = \text{statistical.} \qquad (4)$$

From (1) and (3) we can deduce that an ideal 'elementary structure' is to be represented by a 'mechanical model', and from (2) and (4) that an ideal 'complex structure' is to be represented by a 'statistical model'. In fact, Lévi-Strauss says:

> In primitive societies these laws [marriage rules] can be expressed in models calling for actual grouping of the individuals according

to kin or clan; these are mechanical models. . . . In our own society . . . it would be a statistical model (1958: 311).

So, as it is quite sure that his 'own society' would be classified as a 'complex structure,' we find indeed that:

$$\text{elementary structure} = \text{mechanical model} \qquad (5)$$
$$\text{complex structure} = \text{statistical model.} \qquad (6)$$

When dealing with the criteria of prescription and preference, Lévi-Strauss says that:

The difference between 'prescriptive' and 'preferential' does not appertain to the systems themselves, but to the way in which these systems are conceptualised, according to what I called elsewhere (1958) a 'mechanical' or a 'statistical' model (1965: 18; 1967: xxiii).

Whence we can deduce:

$$\text{prescriptive} = \text{mechanical} \qquad (7)$$
$$\text{preferential} = \text{statistical.} \qquad (8)$$

From (5) and (7), and from (6) and (8), we have:

$$\text{elementary} = \text{prescriptive} \qquad (9)$$
$$\text{complex} = \text{preferential.} \qquad (10)$$

But, since Lévi-Strauss also states that 'an elementary structure can be equally preferential or prescriptive' (1967: xxi), we can further say that:

$$\text{elementary} = \text{preferential.} \qquad (11)$$

From (10) and (11), and from (9) and (11), we arrive in the end at the conclusions:

$$\text{prescriptive} = \text{preferential} \qquad (12)$$
$$\text{elementary} = \text{complex.} \qquad (13)$$

Chapter Four

Terminology and 'Structure': the Dieri Case

I

Les Structures élémentaires de la parenté is generally considered not only as one of the pivots in modern anthropological theory but also as a masterpiece of empirical analysis. We intend to assess its actual virtues in this respect by considering here one of the analyses Lévi-Strauss undertakes. We have chosen the Dieri case in particular because of its importance in earlier anthropological works, and because of the 'anomalous' character that Lévi-Strauss ascribes to it.[1]

As in the case of Wikmunkan society (Lévi-Strauss 1949: 246-51), Lévi-Strauss considers the Dieri system as an example of transition from 'generalized' (asymmetric) exchange to 'restricted' (symmetric) exchange (1949: 260-2).[2] The Dieri system presents, according to Lévi-Strauss, a great many analytical difficulties, mainly due to the fact that it exhibits the 'structure' of a moiety system and the rule of marriage corresponding to a so-called Aranda system (eight sections), namely marriage with the mother's mother's brother's daughter's daughter, or, in general, marriage between children of first cross-cousins, with prohibition of marriage between first cross-cousins (Lévi-Strauss 1949: 256). On the other hand, and in spite of Radcliffe-Brown's efforts, the Dieri system cannot be treated as an Aranda system, says Lévi-Strauss, because it is only 'apparently systematic' and 'contingent lines are needed in order to close a malformed cycle' (Lévi-Strauss 1949: 204).

Lévi-Strauss analyses the Dieri system in chapter XIII of *Les Structures élémentaires de la parenté*, under the heading

---

[1] This is not the only system to which Lévi-Strauss ascribes peculiar characteristics, but it is one of the more revealing for the study of his method.
[2] cf. Needham's analysis of Wikmunkan society (1962b).

'Harmonic and Dysharmonic Regimes', the main argument of which, as we have already seen in chapter 2, relies on the relationship between those regimes and the different types of 'elementary structures'. The relationship posited is that systems of 'generalized exchange' can take place only in 'harmonic regimes' (matrilocal and matrilineal or patrilocal and patrilineal), while systems of 'restricted exchange' correspond to 'disharmonic regimes' (patrilocal and matrilineal, or matrilocal and patrilineal).

The aim of this chapter is to reconsider the Dieri case in order to assess the validity of Lévi-Strauss's interpretation and hypothetical reconstruction of the evolution of the system. The analysis involves the consideration of the logic of a system recognizing four terminological lines and makes it possible, on the other hand, to follow Lévi-Strauss's actual use of his analytical criteria, namely: type of exchange, linearity and locality, and, fundamentally, the role of the so-called kinship terms in the assessment of a 'structure'.

II

The first ethnographic report on the Dieri was published in 1874 by S. Gason, a police trooper working in the Dieri area. Gason was also, together with the missionaries O. Siebert, J. G. Reuther, and H. Vogelsang, one of Howitt's informants. Howitt did his fieldwork among the Dieri around 1870 and after publishing some articles relating to them (Howitt 1878; 1883; 1884b; 1890; 1891) he produced the most complete ethnographical account of the Dieri in his book *The Native Tribes of South-East Australia* (1904). Although there was no further ethnography until Elkin's fieldwork in 1931, the anthropological literature on the Dieri in the first decade of the century is considerable.[3] After the publication of

---

[3] For direction to published sources I have relied in the first place on John Greenway's *Bibliography of the Australian Aborigines and the Native Peoples of Torres Strait to 1959* (1963). This excellent guide was supplemented by titles furnished by Mrs B. Craig, Research Officer, Bibliographical Section of the Australian Institute of Aboriginal Studies, Canberra, who very kindly and efficiently offered further advice on Dieri sources. The Information Officer at Australia House, London, was good enough to provide a photographic copy of Mant's paper (1946). Pastor W. Riedel, Dr T. G. H. Strehlow, and Dr D. Trefry kindly responded to my queries, and Professor A. P. Elkin made many observations from his own point of view on the theoretical framework of this chapter. I am most grateful for the help thus received.

Howitt's works, the theme of 'group marriage' among the Dieri, and the concomitant anthropological theory, aroused the interest of anthropologists such as Lang, Thomas, and Frazer. While Frazer's treatment of the Dieri (1910) is almost a mere repetition of the ethnographical facts provided by Howitt, the works of Lang and Thomas (Lang 1903, 1905; Thomas 1906b) still constitute remarkable pieces of anthropological theory, and their discussions with Howitt (Lang 1907, 1909; Thomas 1906a) did throw light on some obscure points in Dieri ethnography.

Before Elkin's fieldwork, Radcliffe-Brown devoted an article to the analysis of the Dieri relationship terminology (Radcliffe-Brown 1914), and after Elkin's fieldwork and new interpretation of the system (Elkin 1931, 1934, 1938a), Lévi-Strauss included a new analysis of it in *Les Structures élémentaires de la parenté* (1949).

In 1946 the Dieri were reported as numbering fewer than 60 and as being in a state of complete dissolution (Mant 1946: 25). By the time Howitt wrote his *Native Tribes of South-East Australia* (1904), the native tribes of this area were already in a process of rapid disintegration. For this reason Howitt decided to rely only on the ethnographic material gathered before 1889 (Howitt 1904: xiii). Howitt described the Dieri as 'the largest and most important [tribe] occupying country in the Delta of the Barcoo River on the east side of Lake Eyre' (Howitt 1891: 31). According to Gason, they numbered about 230, while the total number of all the groups of Cooper's Creek was estimated by Gason and Howitt at about 1000 to 1200. Among them, the Dieri were reported as 'superior' and according to Howitt they spoke of themselves as the 'fathers' of their neighbouring groups (Howitt 1891: 31).

When referring to the Dieri, Howitt in fact describes the characteristics and social organization of several local groups

> which either recognize a relationship to each other in stock, which is exhibited in their language and in custom, or where the relationship is not acknowledged or has not been ascertained by my informants, it may yet be inferred from the community of custom (Howitt 1891: 31).

Following the information gathered by T. Vogelsang, Berndt describes them as inhabiting the eastern shores and the neighbouring country of Lake Eyre and consisting of two main groups, the Cooper's Creek Dieri or *Ku'na:ri* and the Lake Hope Dieri or

Pandu. These two divisions were bordered by the Ngameni, Jauraworka, and Jantruwanta tribes (Berndt 1939: 167). Dieri territory is reported as deficient in foodstuffs. Dieri hunting activities consisted in the gathering of various species of rats, snakes, and lizards, and owing to the scarcity of these animals their food was principally vegetable (Gason 1879: 259).

It is not possible to gain a clear picture of the physical distribution and exact composition of the local groups. Howitt describes them as follows:

> As an entity it [the Dieri community] is divided into a number of lesser groups, each of which has a name and occupies a definite part of the tribal country. These are again divided and subdivided until we reach the smallest group, consisting of a few families, or even only a single family, which claims also a definite part of the tribal country as its inherited food ground. These groups have local perpetuation through the sons, who inherit the hunting grounds of their fathers (Howitt 1891: 34).

Thus, although it is clear that they were patrilocal, there is not a hint in the above quotation, any more than there is in the rest of the literature, of how these local groups were composed. Taking into account that the inheritance of the totems related to exogamy was matrilineal, to imagine these local groups becomes specially difficult; but with these data it is clearly not possible to think that, as Radcliffe-Brown asserts of Australian societies in general, 'it seems that normally all the persons born in one horde belong to a single line of descent' (Radcliffe-Brown 1931: 105).

They were divided into exogamous moieties, which they called *murdu*. The word in Dieri means 'taste' (Gason 1879: 260) and, according to Gason's vocabulary, in its primary and larger signification it implies 'family' (Gason 1879: 260; cf. Gatti 1930: 107). The accounts of their legends about the creation of their moiety system are somewhat dissimilar. According to Gason, the Dieri believed that their division into exogamous totemic groups belonging to each moiety was created by the *Mura-Mura* (good spirit) in order to prevent the evil effects of intermarriage within a single promiscuous group (Howitt 1904: 480-1). Another informant, O. Siebert, tells the legend as referring to the imposition of exogamy upon already existing moieties, which was decided by the *pinnauru* (elders) because of the same reasons (Howitt 1904:

481; Howitt and Siebert 1904: 129). The discrepancy about whether the Dieri believed in the simultaneous creation of moieties and a system of symmetric alliance, or in the pre-existence of the former over the latter, could just mean that the Dieri actually held both legends; but Siebert's account demonstrates once more that the relationship between sections and a symmetric rule of marriage is not necessary and sufficient.[4] The moieties were named Matteri and Kararu, and, according to Helms, these terms were used 'to distinguish the leading strains of blood' (Helms 1896: 278).

The twenty-six totems designating exogamous groups were inherited from the mother and were divided between the moieties, Kararu and Matteri (Howitt 1904: 91), as follows:

Kararu	*Matteri*
Talara (rain)	Muluru (a caterpillar)
Woma (carpet-snake)	Malura (cormorant)
Kaualka (crow)	Warogati (emu)
Puralko (native companion)	Karawora (eagle-hawk)
Karku (red ochre)	Markara (a fish)
Tidnama (a small frog)	Kuntyiri (*Acacia* sp.)
Kananguru (seed of *Claytonia* sp.)	Kintala (dingo)
Maiaru (a rat)	Yikaura (native cat)
Tapaiuru (a bat)	Kirhapara
Dokubirabira (the pan-beetle)	Kokula (small marsupial)
Milketyelparu	Kanunga (kangaroo-rat)
Kaladiri (a frog)	
Piramoku (the rabbit-bandicoot)	
Punta (shrew mouse)	
Karabana (a small mouse)	

Howitt also provides in his book the corresponding totems of the neighbouring tribes with which the Dieri intermarried. According to the reports there was no correspondence between the totems of the opposite moieties, so the Dieri could marry a person belonging

[4] In this case, the legend demonstrates that the Dieri did not think of their moieties only in terms of the regulation of marriage. The possibility of their pre-existence to their function as exogamous groups shows that their primary function was other than exogamy. Moreover, it demonstrates that sections or moieties could be a convenient division for the purposes of a symmetric system of marriage, but that they are not necessary for the existence of such a system (cf. Elkin 1964: 123; Needham 1960c: 82; 1966: 141).

to any totem group, provided that this totem group was from the opposite moiety, and provided that the person was not a *kami* to Ego.

From the matrilineal inheritance of the totems Howitt concludes that they were 'matriarchal' (Howitt 1891: 36). But this question of descent, defined according to the inheritance of these exogamous totems, gave rise to the first academic discussion related to the Dieri. In spite of Howitt's remarks on the inheritance of totems, Gason, in a letter sent to Frazer, writes:

> The sons take the father's class, the daughters the mother's class, e.g. if a 'dog' (being a man) marries a 'rat' (being a woman) the sons of the issue would be 'dogs', the daughters of the issue would be 'rats' (Gason 1888: 186).

Howitt, who declares that he 'cannot believe [his] eyes' at the sight of Gason's statement, replies that:

> The Dieri said all the children, both girls and boys, take the murdu of their mother and not of the father (Howitt 1890: 90).

The point in dispute was decisive for one of the main theoretical issues at the time, namely, Morgan's hypothesis on the evolution of societies from a matriarchal to a patriarchal stage. Lang, therefore, saw in Gason's alleged mistake a sign of the change in the rule of descent of the Dieri. Gason's confusion arose from the fact that on certain occasions:

> A man gives his totem name to his son, who then has those of both mother and father. This has been done even in the Dieri tribe. Such a practice leads directly to a change in the line of descent (Lang 1909: 284).

Whether the Dieri were changing their 'line of descent' is, according to the evidence, not possible to know, but although Howitt was eagerly trying to test Morgan's ideas, he remained on this point faithful to his ethnographic data. The sons belonged to the same totemic cult groups as their fathers, but these cult totems, unlike the social totems which were inherited from the mothers, had no bearing on marriage and exogamy (Elkin 1938: 50).

Thus an individual belonged to the moiety to which his mother and mother's brother did, and which was transmitted by the inheritance of the mother's totem; and since marriage was patrilocal, he belonged to the local group of his father. Such an organization is also revealed by the fact that:

> the members of the class divisions [i.e. moieties] of the Dieri are distributed over the whole tribal country in the various local groups. The divisions are perpetuated by the children inheriting the class name and the totem name of their mother (Howitt 1891: 36).

Each totemic group had as its head a *pinnauru*, the eldest man of the group belonging to that group, and each local group (horde) had also a *pinnauru*, who could also be the head of the totem. The elders were collectively the heads of the tribe and they decided any communal matters, including marriage arrangements (Howitt 1904: 297-9).

According to Howitt (1904: 160), the Dieri terms of relationship were as in *Table 4*. The term *kaia-kaia* was applied to the mother's mother's mother, who was 'more commonly called *ngandri*, since she is the mother of the *kanini*' (Howitt 1904: 164).

The account of the relationship terminology is incomplete, as Elkin's report demonstrates (Elkin 1931), and contains some obscurities concerning the specifications of the terms *nadada* and *kami* (both rendered as MF); but it permits, nevertheless, the determination of one of the basic features of the Dieri form of classification. The fact that we are dealing with a lineal terminology is indicated by the equations:

$$FF = FFB \ (yenku) \qquad F = FB \ (ngaperi)$$
$$MM = MMZ \ (kanini) \qquad M = MZ \ (ngandri)$$

As Howitt presents it, it is not possible to tell if it is a prescriptive terminology, or, if it is, whether it is symmetric or asymmetric; but the characteristics he gives concerning Dieri institutions suggest the possibility of a symmetric prescriptive terminology. These characteristics are:

1 an explicit prescription of marriage regarding one specific terminological category;
2 exchange of sisters; and
3 reallocation of categories.

Characteristic (1) refers to the rule of marriage concerning the category *nadada*. Howitt refers to a Dieri saying that 'those who are *noa* [potential spouse] are *nadada* to each other' (1904: 163). There was prohibition of marriage between people who were *kami* (genealogically specified as MBC, FZC) to each other, and those who were *nadada* to each other were the children of people who were *kami* to each other. Even if in Howitt's account of the Dieri

Table 4

Howitt's List of Dieri Relationship Terms

1.	*yenku*	FF, FFB, SS
2.	*nadada*	MF, DC
3.	*kami*	MF, DC, MBC, FZC
4.	*kanini*	MM, MMZ, CC, grand-nephew or niece, DC (w.s.)
5.	*ngaperi*	F, FB
6.	*ngandri*	M, MZ, MMM
7.	*papa*]	FZ
8.	*kaka*	MB
9.	*paiara*	WM
10.	*neyi*	eB
11.	*kaku*	eZ
12.	*ngatata*	yB, yZ
13.	*noa*	'potential husband or wife'
14.	*kadi*	WB
15.	*yimari*	WZ
16.	*kamari*	HZ
17.	*buyulu*	MZC
18.	*ngata-mura*	S, D (m.s.)
19.	*ngatani*	S, D (w.s.)
20.	*tidnara*	ZS
21.	*taru*	DH
22.	*kalari*	SW, HM (w.s.)

relationship terminology the term *nadada* applies to individuals (MF, DC), in the second ascending and second descending genealogical levels, the term also applied to individuals of Ego's genealogical level (the children of first cross-cousins). Thus the rule to marry a *nadada* applied to people situated in the same genealogical level and also in alternate levels. This identification of individuals belonging to alternate genealogical levels explains the Dieri practice of marrying the daughter's daughter of an

elder brother (Howitt 1904: 164) and enabled Rivers to compare
the Dieri system with that of Pentecost (Rivers 1914: 58).

Characteristic (2), exchange of sisters, was, according to Howitt
(1904: 161) a concomitant of the *tippa-malku* (i.e. individual) type
of marriage. Howitt distinguished this type of marriage from what
he called *pirrauru* marriage and considered a form of 'group
marriage'. The *tippa-malku* type of marriage was for Howitt the
'individual' marriage among the Dieri and was the result of the
betrothal of a boy and a girl who were in the relation of *noa* to each
other. The betrothal was arranged by the mothers of the children,
who were *kami* to each other, and their brothers, and in every such
case there had to be 'exchange of a sister, own or tribal, of the boy,
who is thereby promised as a wife to the brother, own or tribal,
of the girl' (Howitt 1904: 177).

Characteristic (3) refers to the Dieri practice of changing the
relationship between two women from *kamari* (HZ) to *kami*, in
order to convert their children from *kami* to *noa* and thereby to
allocate them to the marriageable category. Howitt reports that this
was the practice among the Dieri whenever there was not a *noa*
available for a Dieri individual (Howitt 1904: 190). He presents
several examples. In one of them:

> a woman having four sons who were *kami-mara* [*mara* can be
> translated as 'relationship'] to two unmarried girls, it was
> arranged with her and her brethren that one of her sons should
> be placed in the *noa-mara* relation with one of the girls, while
> still remaining in the *kami* relation with the other. . . . Thus
> the *tippa-malku* relation became possible.

In another example (p. 167), he presents the following case:

> two brothers married two sisters, and one had a son and the
> other a daughter. These, being the children of two brothers,
> were brother and sister. Each of them married, and one had a
> son and the other a daughter, who were *kami-mara*. Under the
> Dieri rules these two could not lawfully marry; but since there
> was no girl or woman *noa* to the young man and available, he
> could not get a wife. The respective kindreds, however, got
> over the difficulty by altering the relationship of the two
> mothers from *kamari* (brother's wife) to *kami*, by which change
> the two young people came into the *noa* relationship.

In such cases, the mother-in-law was not called *paiara* but *kami-paiara*, to denote that it was an alteration in the relationship and because all the other relationships involved were not changed.

What the practice demonstrates is the primacy of classification over consanguineal ties, and it relates to prescription in that the same custom can be found in some asymmetric systems (cf. Kruyt 1922: 493).

III

The second discussion relating to Howitt's interpretation of the Dieri system arose from his account of the *pirrauru* relationship. To prove Morgan's ideas it was certainly essential to discover an example of 'group marriage', and because

> the origin of individual marriage, the change of the line of descent, and the final decay of the old class organization are all parts of the same process of social development (Howitt 1888: 34),

it ought presumptively to be found in a society with matrilineal descent and marriage classes. The Dieri were, it was held, such a case. They exhibited a number of supposed symptoms of 'primitive-ness', namely: (1) matrilineal descent, (2) a 'classificatory' termin-ology, and (3) named exogamous moieties. Even though these traits were known to be common in other societies, Howitt saw the Dieri as though it were a singular example of a society which was still in transition from 'group' to 'individual marriage', and saw as an indicator of that transition the fact that the Dieri practised both 'individual' and 'group' marriage.

According to Howitt, the *pirraura* relationship arose from the exchange by brothers of their wives, and thus 'a *pirrauru* is always a "wife's sister" or a "brother's wife",' and 'when two brothers are married to two sisters, they commonly live together in a group-marriage of four' (Howitt 1904: 181). The category of 'marriage-able' women from a 'group marriage' point of view was the same category as in the *tippa-malku* (i.e. individual) form of marriage. In both instances the women had to belong to the opposite moiety and had to be not a *kami* but a *noa* (that is, the daughter of his mother's *kami* and therefore a *nadada* to him). In fact, as Howitt refers to it, a man could have a woman as his *parrauru* provided he was a *noa* to her (Howitt 1904: 181). From data collected by the

missionary Otto Siebert, Howitt interpreted the *kandri* ceremony
as the act by which the heads of the totems allotted the marriageable people of each totem into groups of *pirrauru* (Howitt 1904:
182).

Thus, for Howitt, this example of group marriage was proof of
the hypothesis which stated that classificatory terminologies were
the remnant of a state prior to individual marriage. If 'group
marriage' actually existed, that was a good explanation for classificatory terms. A child applied the term equivalent to our 'mother'
to a group or women, because his or her father had several wives.
The same explanation applied for the equivalent of 'father' and for
each classificatory term. But there were other facts to be explained,
and the possible explanations did not need to follow Morgan's ideas
of the 'undivided commune' and the subsequent 'group marriage'.
'Exogamy' and 'incest prohibitions' had also to be understood, as
well as 'totemism', and for these there was another possible
evolutionary line arising from Darwin's idea that man aboriginally
lived in small communities, each with a single wife. Lang, while
approving Morgan's hypothesis concerning the primacy of matrilineal descent over patrilineal descent, followed Darwin's hypothesis of the historical universality of individual marriage (Lang
1905: vii; 1911: 404) and, together with Thomas, saw the practice
of the *pirrauru* among the Dieri (or the equivalent *piranguru*
among the Arabana) as a later development of individual marriage
and, moreover, not classifiable as 'marriage' at all (Lang 1905:
35-58). Moreover, as Thomas observed, 'if there was a period of
group marriage there was also one of group motherhood' (Thomas
1906b: 123).

This approach was able to elucidate the meaning of classificatory
terms from a very different point of view. Modern conceptions of
relationship terminologies approve Lang's and Durkheim's view of
the problem rather than the line of interpretation derived from
Morgan,[5] about which Lang says:

> the friends of group and communal marriage keep unconsciously
> forgetting, . . . that *our* ideas of sister, brother, father, mother,
> and so on, have nothing to do . . . with the native terms, which
> *include*, indeed, but do not *denote* these relationships as under-
> stood by us (Lang 1903: 100-1; original emphasis).

[5] cf. Needham 1960d: 96-101; 1964a: 23.

E

One demonstration of this proposal was to be found in the Dieri use of their relationship terminology. The fact that the term *kami*, for instance, denoted for the Dieri more a certain status than consanguineal ties is shown by the practice, mentioned above, of reallocating individuals to different categories. When a man could not find a *noa* available for betrothal to him, his mother and another woman who was a *kamari* (HZ; BW) to her were made *kami* by their brothers, so that their children should become *noa* to each other. Howitt adds that this practice was a common one among the Deiri.

Going back to the *pirrauru* relationship, Gason's first translation of the term was 'paramour' (Gason 1879: 303), and this was also Lang's interpretation: *pirrauru* were 'legal paramours' and their existence denoted for him a more advanced rather than a more primitive trait (Lang 1905: 50-8). What kind of an institution it was is difficult to tell just by looking at the ethnography, because even the *kandri* ceremony, which was described by Howitt in 1904 as the allotment of the *pirrauru* groups, was described by him in 1907 as:

> the *kandri* ceremony announces the 'betrothal', as I call it, of a male and a female *noa*, no more and no less (Howitt 1907: 179).

Thus the ceremony was related by Howitt to both 'group' and 'individual' (*tippa-malku*) marriages. The evidence Howitt gives actually fits better with Lang's interpretation, and what Howitt called 'group marriage' was probably the fact that groups of brothers with their individual wives lived in the same local group. Within those groups every classificatory brother was a *noa* to each one of his brother's wives. It is probable then that the term *pirrauru* denoted those individuals who were marriageable to each other and lived together in a local group, because what seems to be true, as Thomas says, is that even if all the *pirrauru* had to be *noa* to each other, not all the *noa* people were *pirrauru* to each other. So for any individual the *noa* groups was wider than the *pirrauru* group (Thomas 1907: 308).

It could also be plausible, then, that both interpretations given by Howitt to the *kandri* ceremony were valid, and that therefore the ceremony served two purposes for the Dieri, namely: (i) to establish 'individual' (*tippa-malku*) marriages, and (ii) to indicate which groups of *noa* were going to live in the same local group after marriage. But what seems to be indisputable is Thomas's demonstration that the *pirrauru* relationship – even if it was, as Howitt saw it, a kind of 'group marriage' – still did not explain the use of classificatory terms, because Howitt in one passage talks about the 'application of the term *ngaperi* (father) to the other brothers who have not become *pirrauru*'. As Thomas specifies, they applied the term *ngaperi* 'to all the men of the *noa* group' (Thomas 1907: 309). Hence, for the use of the classificatory term *ngaperi*, the only fact that the Dieri needed to take into account was who were the 'marriageable' (*noa*) men for their mothers, regardless of the consideration whether they were *pirrauru* to their mothers or not.

In taking the *pirrauru* relationship as the example of 'group marriage' Howitt did not follow Fison's definition of the term. For Fison, in the expression 'group marriage':

> the word 'marriage' itself has to be taken in a certain modified sense. . . . It does not necessarily imply actual giving in marriage or cohabitation; what it implies is a marital right, or rather a marital qualification, which comes with birth (Fison 1893: 689).

According to this definition, Howitt did not need to use the *pirrauru* relationship in order to present an example of 'group marriage'. He could just look at the characteristic of the Dieri system described by himself as:

> a boy at his birth acquires a marital right as regard those women of the other class-name who are not forbidden to him under the restrictions arising from consanguinity (Howitt 1883: 457; cf. 1904: 165).

Fison was therefore looking for a quite different kind of institution than the *pirrauru* marriage as described for Howitt. As Needham says:

> in the last quarter of the nineteenth century the study of what was taken to be 'group marriage' in Australia brought into prominence an institution which Durkheim named 'connubium' and has more recently been termed *prescriptive alliance* (Needham 1964c: 125-6).

Considering 'group marriage' in this way, it is quite clear that: (1) among the Dieri the alliance system was certainly a prescriptive one, and (2) Lang's and Fison's apparently so different conceptions of 'classificatory' terms need not be explained as deriving from consanguineal ties, and (3) within the different modes of social classification, prescriptive terminologies constitute a definite type which corresponds symbolically to the idea of 'connubium' between categorically defined groups or persons.

IV

In 1914 Radcliffe-Brown devoted an article to the consideration of obscurities and possible errors in Howitt's account of the Dieri relationship terminology (Radcliffe-Brown 1914). He first pointed out certain defects in Howitt's analysis of the genealogy presented facing p. 159 of *The Native Tribes of South-East Australia* (1904). Howitt's statement that an individual stands in the position of *kaka*, MB, to another because he is *ngaperi*, F, to him, is obviously wrong (Howitt 1904: 166). Radcliffe-Brown gives two more instances (p. 53) in which Howitt makes the same sort of mistake, and finally examines Howitt's specification of the terms *nadada* and *kami*, both rendered as mother's father (Howitt 1904: 160-2). Radcliffe-Brown thought the identification of the two terms was a possible error and suggested a correction: the term *nadada* should be specified as father's mother and father's mother's brother, but also 'in a looser and more extended sense' as mother's father (1914: 54). He claimed that in this way it was easier to understand the Dieri saying that 'those who are *noa* are *nadada* to each other', because:

> I am the younger brother (*ngatata*) to my father's father's sister, and she is *nadada* (father's mother) to the woman I call *noa*. It follows that as I am brother to the *nadada* of my *noa* I am *nadada* to the latter and she is *nadada* to me (Radcliffe-Brown 1914: 54).

If this suggestion were accepted, the Dieri system would be, said Radcliffe-Brown, 'wonderfully simple and logical and quite in agreement with other systems in Australia' (1914: 54), so he drew a table (*Figure 6*) showing a system of relationship which, according to him, proved 'the existence of the four matrimonial classes in the Dieri tribe' (1914: 56). By 'matrimonial classes' he meant, as he explained, 'divisions of a tribe such as those named Ippai, Kubbi,

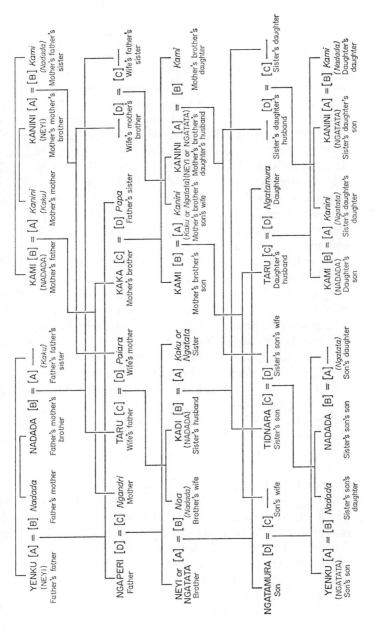

Figure 6 Radcliffe-Brown's representation of the Dieri relationship terminology (Racliffe-Brown 1914: 55)

Kumbo and Murri in the Kamilaroi tribe' (p. 56, n.; cf. Fison and
Howitt 1880: 42; Howitt 1904: 201). He pointed out in a footnote
that many writers (such as Howitt, Frazer, Thomas, Schmidt),
assumed the non-existence of four matrimonial classes because in
some tribes those classes were not named (as in the case of the
Dieri). 'There is not a scrap of evidence at present for the existence
in Australia of any tribe which has not four divisions of this kind.'
The four classes, he claimed, 'certainly do exist' among the Dieri.

But if they were not named, and their existence was simply
deduced by Radcliffe-Brown from the composition of the relationship terminology, why should anybody call these inferential
constructs 'classes'? Moreover, if 'class' was the term he employed
to denote a certain possible arrangement of relationship terms in a
diagram representing a system, why employ the term 'class' at all
and not refer to that arrangement to classify the system? If
systems had to be classified into different 'class' types, whether
the classes 'were named or not', then the classification denoted a
categorization of systems of 'classes' the indicators of which were
to be found in possible arrangements of the relationship terms, no
matter whether or not the classes actually existed. One wonders
why one should not classify the systems directly by the composition
of their relationship terminologies, and then just provide the
ethnographical information on whether or not a particular society
with a particular terminological system possessed a corresponding
set of marriage classes.

Anyhow, some years later, in *The Social Organization of
Australian Tribes*, Radcliffe-Brown represents the Dieri as having
instead 'a kinship system of the Aranda type' (1931: 48). If so,
however, why are they not included there under the heading
'Aranda type' (p. 74) but are instead classified separately as the
'Dieri type'? It seems quite arbitrary to consider that a system
which does not possess named classes, but has a terminology
consistent with a 'four-class' system, possesses in fact 'classes'
that are not named, and then not to follow the same reasoning
when a society possesses no sections but has a 'kinship system'
conforming to an 'eight-section' type.

In 1951 Radcliffe-Brown deals again with the Dieri system, but
this time the Dieri have for him 'a highly organized system of
double descent' (1951: 40), derived from the existence of patrilineal
totemic groups (*pintara*) and matrilineal totemic clans (*madu*).

According to him, the Dieri are in close association with the matrilineal totem of the father. As they are also, he says, in a close association with the patrilineal totemic clan of the father's father and with the matrilineal clans of the mother and the father's mother, each Dieri individual seems to be connected with all possible totemic groups in the Dieri community. On the basis of the available ethnography, however, the interpretation of the Dieri system as a system of 'double descent' is very difficult to prove. The *pintara* totem that sons inherited from the father was of a very different nature from the cult totem inherited from the mother. Only the matrilineal totem was related to exogamy, because 'flesh and blood' were inherited from the mother. The *pintara* they received from the father was related instead to locality and war (cf. Elkin 1938: 50).

V

As a matter of fact, there was a mistake in Howitt's account of the Dieri relationship terminology, but not in the respect that Radcliffe-Brown sought to correct. From his own fieldwork, Elkin provided a full account of the terminology which is consistent with Howitt's report, except for the specification of the term *kami* (Elkin 1931: 494; 1938a: 49). The correct specification for *kami* was father's mother, and that for *nadada* was mother's father (see *Table 5*), and as Elkin remarks: 'In Howitt's list there would be no term for father's mother if the "mother's father" [which Howitt gave as the specification of both *kami* and *nadada*] is not regarded as a simple transposition of words' (1938: 49; cf. *Figure 7*). Elkin describes the system as having certain features in common with the Aranda type, namely: reckoning of descent through four lines, the use of four terms in the second ascending genealogical level, prohibition of marriage between first cross-cousins, and a rule of marriage with second cross-cousins. He notes, however, some differences from an Aranda system, for instance the fact that in an Aranda system cross-cousins are classified with MMBW, while among the Dieri they are classified with FM (*kami*).

The table by which Elkin represents the Dieri relationship terminology shows one of the characteristics of the system regarding certain categories in the first ascending, the first descending, and Ego's genealogical level: some positions are denoted by two terms (*tidnara-taru, ngatamura-paiera, nadada-noa, nadada-kadi*); one of these denotes potential affines and the other actual affines. WM, for instance, is categotically a *ngatamura* to Ego, that is the daughter of one of Ego's *nadada* and the mother of one of

Table 5

Elkin's Account of Dieri Relationship Terms

1.	*yenku*	FF, FFZ, MMBSS, MMBSD, SS, SD, ZSDH, ZSSW
2.	*nadada*	MF, MFZ, MMBW, WMM, WMMB, W, MMBDD, MFZDD, WB, DC
3.	*kami*	FM, FMB, WFF, FZS, FZD, MBS, MBD, ZSS, ZSD
4.	*kanini*	MM, MMB, WMF, WMFZ, MFZH, ZDS, ZDD
5.	*ngapari*	F, FB
6.	*ngandri*	M, MZ
7.	*papa*	FZ, MBW
8.	*kaka*	MB, FZH
9.	*tidnara*	FFZC, ZC
10.	*taru*	WF, SW, DH, DHZ
11.	*paiera*	WM, WMB, ZDH
12.	*ngatamura*	MMBC, S, D
13.	*niyi*	eB, WZH
14.	*kaku*	eZ, WBW
15.	*ngatata*	yB, WZH, yZ, WBW
16.	*noa*	W, H
17.	*kadi*	WB
18.	*kalari*	ZSW

Ego's *nadada*, but because she is the mother of Ego's actual *noa* (W), she becomes *paiera* to Ego.

Another characteristic of the system is that each of the terms that denote actual and classificatory brothers and sisters (*niyi*; *kaku*) is added to the term *yenku*, at Ego's genealogical level, to denote the people of Ego's genealogical level who belong to Ego's moiety but not Ego's line.

Elkin also reports that 'the Dieri is no exception to the Australian custom of the betrothal and marriage of young girls to men much older than themselves; the difference may be about thirty years', and he adds that 'the two persons concerned usually belong to alternate generations, as when there is an exchange of sister's daughters between two men who are related as man and wife's

Figure 7 Elkin's representation of the Dieri relationship terminology (Elkin 1931: 497)

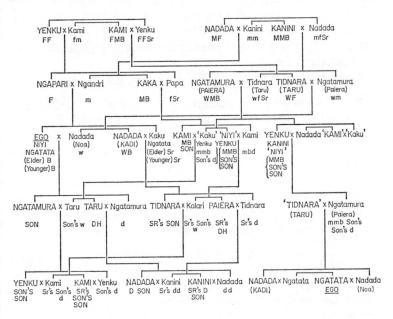

x Joins husband and wife

⌐——⌐ Joins brother and sister

| Joins parents and children

Terms in [brackets] are those that result from betrothal

Inverted commas show that the relationship is not 'own', but only legal

Capital letters denote males

Small letters denote females

mother's brother' (1938a: 58). Because the Dieri identify categories belonging to the same line and in alternate genealogical levels, such marriages between old men and young girls are easy to understand. A Dieri man marries a girl who is a *nadada* to him and the daughter of a woman who is *ngatamura* to him. But *ngatamura* is a term that designates positions in the first ascending and the first descending genealogical levels of the *nadada* line, and the spouses necessarily therefore belong either to the same genealogical level or to alternate levels. Marriage between people who belong to different genealogical levels seems to be qualified in one respect: the husband belongs to the higher genealogical level and the wife to the lower (Howitt 1904: 177). Another qualification seems to be that, in the case of a man who marries his BDD (who is a *nadada* to him), he has to be *ngatata* to his brother (*niyi*), i.e. he has to be categorically the younger brother of his wife's mother's father (Howitt 1904: 177).

Concerning this trait of the Dieri system, Elkin writes:

> just as I can marry the daughter's daughter of the *kanini* who is my mother's mother's brother, so too I may marry the daughter's daughter of this *kanini*, that is my mother's mother's brother's son's son's daughter's daughter. . . . Professor Radcliffe-Brown has previously suggested that this was the type of grandchild who would be married according to most systems of the Aranda type, including probably the Dieri. She is the daughter's daughter of a moiety brother, and it is customary for a man to marry a woman so related to him (Elkin 1938: 60).

As I said above, marriage with a *nadada* of a lower genealogical alternate level is consistent with the Dieri mode of classification, but this category did not include the MMBSSDD (who was in fact a *kami* to Ego) nor was the MMBSSDD included in the same category as BDD. In the Dieri relationship terminology the specifications of *nadada* are, in fact, MMBDD at Ego's level, and BDD or MBDDDD in the second descending level, as a consequence of the four matrilines and the alternation by genealogical level. On this point Elkin confuses the identification of categories in alternate levels derived from a terminology with four patrilines, as in the Aranda, with that derived from four matrilines, as in the Dieri.

Elkin's report of the moiety system and the matrilineal totemic clans is entirely consistent with Howitt's account, but Elkin adds some relevant information regarding the role of the father among the Dieri. According to him, the Dieri considered that a child inherited his flesh and blood from his mother but still maintained a close and important relationship with his father. It was the father who cared for the child, was head or senior of the local group to which the child belonged, and was very much concerned with the initiation of his son or the marriage of his daughter, but what was more important, says Elkin, is that the father's cult totem was passed on to his fully initiated son. It included a sacred and secret complex of mythology, site, and ritual (Elkin 1931: 497).

VI

Lévi-Strauss's analysis of the Dieri system is based on Elkin's report of their relationship terms. From the rest of the literature on the Dieri he only mentions, apart from Elkin's works (1931, 1940), two works by Radcliffe-Brown (1914, 1931). There is not in his analysis any reference to Gason, Howitt, or any of the earlier ethnographic reports (cf. below, Appendix).

He considers as the relevant characteristics for an appraisal of the system the fact that the Dieri possessed:

1 matrilineal moieties,
2 matrilineal totemic clans,
3 no apparent sections or subsections,
4 a rule of the Aranda type (prohibition of marriage between first cross-cousins and 'preferential marriage between the four types of second cousins descended from cross-cousins'),
5 reciprocal terms between members of the second ascending generation and the second descending generation,
6 FFZ and MFZ are classified with, or may actually be, FMBW and MMBW respectively (Lévi-Strauss 1949: 256).

Although characteristics (4), (5), and (6) are consistent with an Aranda system, Lévi-Strauss gives the following facts as the main differences between this system and that of the Dieri:

7 cross-cousins are classified with FM and FMB (*kami*),
8 MMB ≠ MMBSS (*kanini* and *niyi* respectively, while the Aranda have just one term for both),
9 there are only sixteen terms (and 'this has no correlation whatsoever with the Aranda terminology or with the Kariera terminology or with the figure which might be calculated, on the basis of these two last, for a simple moiety system' [Lévi-Strauss 1949: 256]).

Looking at Elkin's table, says Lévi-Strauss (1949: 256), it is clear that one cannot regard the Dieri system as an Aranda one, and he then remarks that certain identifications are possible, namely:

10 *tidnara* = *taru* (by marriage),
11 *ngatamura* = *paiera* (by marriage),
12 *ngatata* = *yenku* ('passing through' *kaku*, *yenku*'s sister and *kami*'s wife).

Figure 8 Lévi-Strauss's 'simplified' representation of the Dieri system (1949: 260, Figure 40)

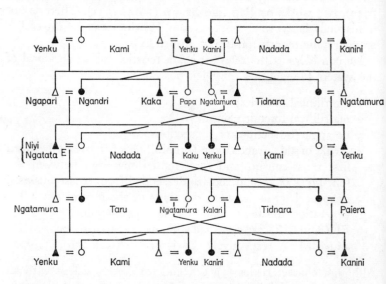

From these data, Lévi-Strauss presents first a 'simplified' representation of the Dieri system consisting of four patrilineal lines and restricted exchange between children of cross-cousins (see *Figure 8*). He finds in this diagram, however, a series of anomalies, which indeed he attributes to the system. He tries to answer then: (i) whence the dichotomy preventing marriage of first cross-cousins arose,[6] and (ii) how the terms *yenku*, *nadada*, *kami*, and *ngatamura* 'circulate' through several lines.

[6] R. Needham points out that, by a slip at some point in the preparation of the English edition, the original *d'où*, whence, was misrendered as 'when' (1969:206).

In an attempt to solve these problems he proposes as a working hypothesis the following possible evolution of the system (*Figure 9*). In addition to this, Lévi-Strauss considers the Dieri system as

Figure 9 Reconstruction of the hypothetical evolution of the Dieri system according to Lévi-Strauss (1949: 261, Figure 41)

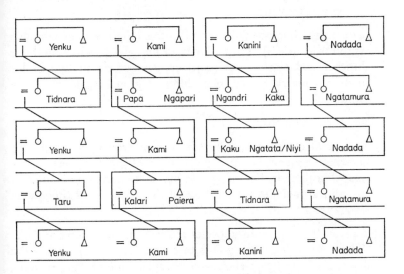

having changed from a 'harmonic' regime and a 'matrilateral' system (1949: 275) to its present-day form, 'an apparent form of eight subsection *structure*,' under the influence of disharmonic regimes. In the present-day form of the Dieri system 'the patrilateral and the matrilateral systems act concurrently' (1949: 275).

VII

In 1962, Lane and Lane, in a paper dealing with the problem of implicit double descent, reconsidered Radcliff-Brown's interpretation of the Dieri system as a system of double descent.

They point out (p. 50) that Radcliffe-Brown's claim of double descent for the Dieri, based on the notion of double clan affiliation, is unacceptable according to the available ethnography. Elkin has repeatedly pointed out, they say, that the ceremonial totem called *pintara* (which Radcliff-Brown takes as the 'patrilineal clan') has nothing to do with marriage. But they claim that the Dieri system can still be considered as a system of double descent 'in the sense of the occurrence of implicit patrilineal moieties intersecting the matrisibs' (1962: 50). Although they do not present an analysis of the Dieri terminology, they state that it is consistent with an arrangement by which:

> a man and his mother's mother's brother (alternating generations within a matrisib) marry women of one group, while mother's brother and sister's son (adjacent generations to Ego in his matrisib) marry women of a different group (Lane and Lane 1962: 50).

They then claim that:

> the result of differentiating adjacent generations and equating alternate generations in a given matrisib on the basis of the matrilineal affiliation of the father is to create two implicit patrilineal moieties intersecting all the matrisibs of the system (1962: 50).

However, 'these patrilineal cycles received no overt recognition'.

There are at least two points to consider here: (1) what is the relevance of a concept such as an 'implicit intersecting moiety', and (2) what exactly is the meaning of 'matrisib' in Lane and Lane's article.

On page 47 of their article they state that 'by intersecting moiety' they mean 'a dichotomous division which bisects every component sib of the society'. Among the Dieri, the 'patrilineal cycles received no overt recognition', so they constitute 'implicit patrilineal moieties'. It is possible to apply to their argument the same sort of criticism that they apply to Radcliffe-Brown's interpretation: among the Dieri there is no recognition of any patrilineal principle in relation to marriage. What the Dieri have is a rule that prescribes marriage with the category *nadada* and it is the particular conformation of their relationship terminology which has the effect that men belonging to the same matrilineal line but to alternate levels marry in the same line of the opposite moiety. To call this consequence of the constitution of the relationship terminology an 'implicit patrilineal moiety' or to call it 'implicit patrilineal clans' does not make any difference: neither of these phrases corresponds to any actual institution in Dieri society or to any principle that the Dieri apply in their particular mode of classification.

As for the 'sibs' which these 'patrilineal moieties' intersect, are they matrilineal terminological lines or actual matrilineal institutions such as, for example, the matrilineal totemic groups? It seems that for Lane and Lane they are actual matrilineal institutions; otherwise, the phrase 'the Dieri kinship terminology was consistent with their system of matrilineal sibs' (1962: 50) would be a tautology. The Dieri, however, did not marry a person because she or he belonged to a certain 'matrilineal sib', but because she or he was in a certain categorical relationship (*nadada*) to them. The distinction between marriageable and non-marriageable people was based upon a terminological distinction, and membership of a certain matrilineal totemic group was only a secondary device specially useful in cases of marriage between people belonging to different tribes.

VIII

At this point we may revert to Lévi-Strauss's account of the system. It will be remembered that he isolates certain characteristics as evidence of the systematic difference between the Dieri and the Aranda forms of organization. Let us consider first those characteristics which we have listed as (7) and (8), namely, cross-cousins are classified with FM and FMB (while among the Aranda they are classified with MMBW); MMB ≠ MMBSS (*kanini* and *yenku* respectively, while the Aranda have just one term for both).

From the point of view of the configuration of the relationship terminology, what is meant by an 'eight-section system' is a prescriptive terminology that consists of four lines and expresses a rule by which the category that contains the genealogical specification of second cross-cousins is prescribed. This factor is revealed by the repetition of the same term in alternate levels within a single line. Thus, if one considers a terminology that contains patrilines, the diagram that can be drawn is as follows (cf. *Figure 10*). In a terminology of this kind, it is perfectly clear why the category that contains the specification of first cross-cousin is designated by the same term as the category genealogically specified as mother's mother's brother's wife and her brother. The categories belong to the same terminological line and to alternate genealogical levels. The same can be said about the category that contains MMB and the one that contains MMBSS: there is no need for more than one term for both because they belong to the same terminological line in alternate genealogical levels.

Figure 10 Diagram of a four-line symmetric prescriptive terminology (patrilines)

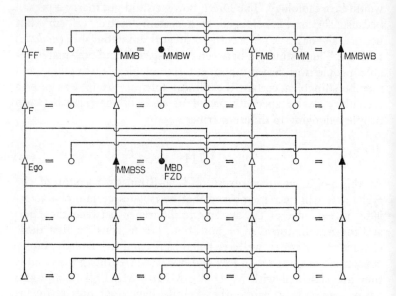

If, instead of being based on patrilines, a four-line symmetric prescriptive terminology is based on matrilines, the diagram is the following one (see *Figure 11*). In a terminology of this sort, the category that contains the specification of first cross-cousins does not belong to the line containing the specification for MMBW, but to the line to which the specifications of FM and FMB belong. On the other hand, MMB and MMBSS are contained in categories that do not belong to the same terminological line either.

If the Dieri terminology differs from an 'Aranda terminology' in the points Lévi-Strauss indicates (and which we have numbered

Figure II Diagram of a four-line symmetric prescriptive terminology (matrilines)

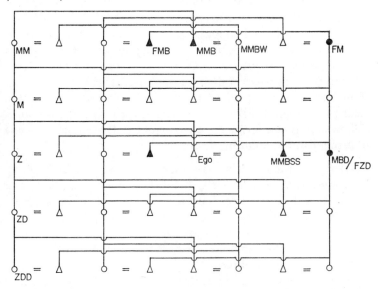

Figure I2 Dieri relationship terminology (according to Elkin's list of terms, cf. *Table 5*)

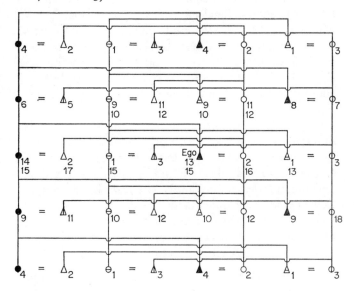

F

as 7 and 8), this could be due to the fact that what is meant by an 'Aranda terminology' is a terminology based on four patrilines, whereas the Dieri terminology is probably based on four matrilines. This is the first consideration we are going to take into account in our analysis of the system.

Let us then see whether the Dieri terminology is consistent with a four-line symmetric prescriptive terminology based on matrilines. Taking into account Elkin's list of terms, the resulting diagram is as shown above (see *Figure 12*). Looking at the diagram it is possible to distinguish the following features:

(i) there are four matrilines headed by the terms *yenku*, FFZ (1); *kami*, FM (3); *nadada*, MFZ (2); and *kanini*, MM (4);

(ii) in each line these four terms are applied in alternate genealogical levels (only in Ego's line at Ego's level 0 there are distinctive terms for older and younger brother and for older and younger sister, but these are common features in lineal terminologies);

(iii) in the first ascending and the first descending genealogical levels the term *tidnara* (9) designates the category of persons who belong to the same moiety as Ego and who do not belong to the categories F, M, FZ, MB. The term *taru* (10) denotes affinal status: it designates the actual WF, who is genealogically *tidnara* to Ego, in the first ascending genealogical level, and also the category of marriageable persons for Ego's children in the first descending genealogical level (in other words, persons of the first descending genealogical level who belong to Ego's moiety but not to Ego's line);

(iv) setting aside exceptions to be enumerated below, the basic differentiations between categories are made according to genealogical line and level, but not according to sex. The exceptions to this rule are found in only the first ascending and the first descending levels, as shown in *Figure 13*.

(v) as we noted above, *tidnara-taru*, *ngatamura-paiera*, *nadada-noa*, and *nadada-kadi*, in the first ascending and in Ego's genealogical level, are terms denoting respectively, in each pair, potential and actual affines in these positions.

Let us consider the formal diagram employed above (*Figure 11*) to represent a four-line symmetric prescriptive terminology, and then relate the features of the Dieri relationship terminology to that diagram.

The diagram is composed of two divisions, each of which contains two lines. There are in the diagram two kinds of connection: vertical connections between points located in each level, and horizontal connections between the points of each line with points located in the lines of the other division. Considering a single line, the points at alternate levels are connected by equation signs with points of a single line of the other division. Each line is composed of two kinds of signs, namely a circle and a triangle, in each level.

Figure 13 Categories of the same genealogical level and line differentiated by sex (according to Elkin's list of terms, cf. *Table 5*)

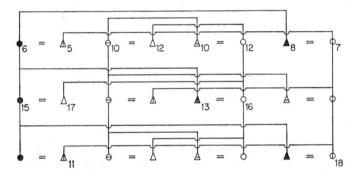

Each of these elements has a correlate in a four-line symmetric prescriptive terminology. The vertical lines correspond to terminological lines, each point in a line corresponds to a genealogically definable term, each level to a genealogical level; each equation sign corresponds to a genealogically necessary connection between terms; circle and triangle correspond to terms of the same line and the same genealogical level defined genealogically as siblings of opposite sex. Operationally one can define a four-line symmetric prescriptive terminology as a terminology the elements of which conform to a diagram such as that described above.

The characteristics numbered (i) and (ii) of the Dieri relationship terminology show that it contains the main indicators of a terminology as defined above. There are four matrilines and in each of them the terms corresponding to Ego's genealogical level are repeated in the second ascending and the second descending genealogical levels within the same lines. In order to analyse the first ascending and the first descending genealogical levels, it is necessary to take into account that, to be consistent with the diagram we are considering, the terminology ought to possess a clear indication that each line is related to the line in the other terminological division which does not contain the terms to which those of Ego's line are related at Ego's level and at the second ascending and descending genealogical levels. Looking at the diagram representing the Dieri terminology (*Figure 12*) it is possible to see that there is an indication of that sort denoted by the following facts: (*a*) the terms employed in the first ascending and the first descending levels do not repeat any of the terms of the other levels; (*b*) the four lines are constantly distinguished; and (*c*) each line is related to the line of the opposite terminological division where the terms of the genealogical level previously considered are not related.

Although the Dieri terminology is, as we have seen, entirely consistent with the diagram representing a four-line symmetric prescriptive terminology, it could be said that it is not consistent in the most economical possible way. The differentiations by sex in the first ascending and the first descending genealogical levels are not necessary if one considers the logic of the diagram itself. The explanation, therefore, is not to be found by looking at the diagram and the relations and differentiations it implies. If the explanation is not to be found in the logic underlying a totally formal analysis of the terminology, it presumably lies in the relationship between the mode of classification represented by the terminology and the actual rules and the social forms coexisting with the terminology in Dieri society.

Before going on with the analysis let us make some assumptions explicit. Terminologies represent modes of social classification which are susceptible of analysis according to entirely formal criteria, such as (*a*) linearity/non-linearity, (*b*) prescription/non-prescription, (*c*) symmetry/asymmetry. These criteria are the formal consequences of basic principles of classification which can be applied, systematically or not, to different analytical spheres of social organization. If the principles are consistently applied, one is likely to find systematic correspondences between any two possible spheres. In the Dieri case, the terminological divisions actually correspond to the exogamous moieties. The correspondence, nevertheless, does not permit the inference of any causal connection between the two spheres, mainly because if there is a causal connection it is not a necessary one. This is demonstrated by the fact that (i) there are societies that possess a terminology divided symmetrically and do not possess exogamous moieties (as in the case of Sinhalese society [see Leach 1960: 124-5]); (ii) there are societies that possess exogamous moieties and do not have a symmetric terminology (as in the case of Mota society [see Needham 1960d: 23-9; 1964b: 302-14]).

These considerations lead to two basic issues in the discussion of the relationship between terminologies and other spheres of social organization, namely: (*a*) the relationship between symmetric prescriptive terminologies and the existence of 'marriage classes' (viz. moieties, sections, and subsections), and (*b*) the relationship between terminological differentiations that are not logically related to any specific form of terminology but to rules or social forms coexistent with them.

Considering the Dieri terminology and Dieri social forms, the exogamous moieties permitted a classification of Dieri individuals that was entirely consistent with the classification derived from the terminological divisions. But there did not exist in Dieri society, so far as can be seen from the ethnographical reports, any social forms comparable with the exogamous moieties and consistent with the terminological classification into four lines. In other words, there were neither subsections nor any other form of actual institutions corresponding to the four lines in the terminology. The non-existence of subsections has, nevertheless, nothing to do with the formal definition of the Dieri terminology as a four-line symmetric prescriptive terminology.[7] All that can be said in this respect is that there is no correspondence between the terminological classification of persons into four lines and a particular correlated set of social institutions. This fact did not prevent the Dieri from having a rule of marriage consistent with a classification into four terminological lines. The rule was based on categorical distinctions, and the whole system worked like an 'eight-subsection system', only these subsections are not a necessary concomitant of the four lines and the rule of marriage.

---

[7] cf. Dumont 1964; Needham 1966, 1967a, 1969, on the relationship between formal features of a terminology and empirical institutions.

In the case of the differentiations by sex in the first ascending and the first descending genealogical levels of the Dieri relationship terminology, we are confronted with a problem of a different kind. Those differentiations are not necessary formal features of a four-line symmetric prescriptive terminology. They cannot be derived from the logical configuration of such a terminology. Instead, they can be related to rules and institutions of Dieri society.

The differentiation between the genealogical specifications of mother and mother's brother (*ngandri* and *kaka*) and between those of father and father's sister (*ngaperi* and *papa*), although both pairs of terms contain categories belonging to the same terminological line, is a common trait of lineal terminologies and is probably accounted for by the special roles of the people categorized as such regarding Ego. *Ngandri* is the term that denotes the actual mother, her sisters, and all the women of the same line and genealogical level as these (they are *ngandri-waka* for Ego, cf. Howitt 1891: 45-9).[8] They are the women of Ego's exogamous totemic group, and probably most of them live in the same patrilocal group as Ego. They are all of them 'same flesh and blood' as Ego. This also applied to individuals categorized as *kaka* (MB, FZH), but they certainly lived in a different local group, because locality was decided patrilineally. On the other hand, individuals categorized as *kaka* had an important role concerning Ego's marriage: one of them was, together with Ego's actual *ngandri*, M, the person who arranged Ego's betrothal and they were also the fathers of Ego's *kami* (the prohibited category).

The women categorized as *papa* (father's sisters) were the mothers of Ego's *kami*. They were same 'flesh and blood' as Ego's father and they lived in the same local groups as Ego's *kaka*, MB. Whether *kami* was the prohibited category because the women categorized as such were 'same flesh and blood' as Ego's *ngaperi*, F, and therefore a patrilineal principle was added to the matrilineal inheritance of 'flesh and blood', or whether the prohibition of marriage with a *kami* was borrowed by the Dieri from neighbouring societies,[9] so that the distinction between *ngaperi* and *papa* could

[8] According to Gatti's vocabulary (1930), the translation of *waka* is 'small' ('piccolo', 'basso', p. 115).
[9] Howitt thought that marriage with a *nadada* was borrowed by the Dieri from neighbouring tribes (Howitt 1904: 189) and that previously the prescribed category was *kami*. This hypothesis makes sense only on the improbable assumption that a whole type of terminology was adopted.

be seen as a functional one regarding that prohibition, it is impossible to know. Durkheim would doubtless have explained the prohibition to marry a *kami* as a result of matrilineal descent and patrilineal residence: Ego's *kami* lived in the same local groups as Ego's *kaka* (MB) and thus were 'too near' to Ego because they were 'too near' to Ego's matrilineal totemic ceremonies (Durkheim 1898: 18-19; 1902: 100-12; see *Figure 14*). Although this explanation

Figure 14 Hypothetical distribution of Dieri categories among local groups (according to Elkin's list of terms, cf. *Table 5*)

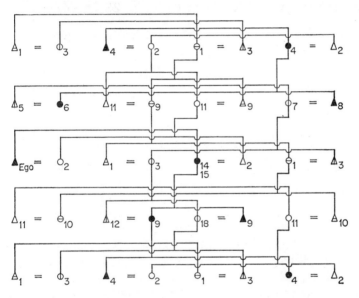

does not apply to other systems presenting similar characteristics (such as the Aranda and the Mara), it is plausible for the Dieri. The distinctions between *ngandri* (M, MZ) and *kaka* (MB), and between *ngaperi* (F, FB) and *papa* (FZ), were probably useful for the Dieri in considering the people involved in the betrothal and regarding the prohibited category (*kami*).

The terms in the first descending genealogical level are more difficult to explain. According to Elkin's diagram the set of terms for this level is composed of: *tidnara*, ZS, ZD (9); *taru*, SW, DH (10); *ngatamura*, S, D (12); *paiera*, ZDH (11); and *kalari*, ZSW (18).

The first puzzling feature is the application of the term *tidnara* (which in the first ascending genealogical level belongs to the *yenku* line) to positions in the *kanini* line at this level (cf. *Table 6*). Why is there this change of line in this particular genealogical level, if there is not any other term that is allocated to more than one line? If the principle of alternation were followed consistently at this level, the terms for the positions concerned (ZS, ZD) would logically be *ngandri* (M)[10] and *kaka* (MB), i.e. the terms denoting the same positions in the first ascending genealogical level. But there is no doubt that these terms are not repeated in the first descending level, and, furthermore, the term *tidnara* is specified as 'nephew' by Gason (1879), as ZS by Vogelsang (in

Table 6 Dieri relationship terms by genealogical level (according to Elkin's list, cf. *Table 5*)

Genealogical level	Relationship terms																	
	1	2	3	4	5	6	7	8	9	10	11	12	13	14	15	16	17	18
+2	+	+	+	+									[+]	[+]	[+]			
+1					+	+	+	+	+	+	+	+						
0	+	+	+	[+]										+	+	+	+	+
−1						+	+	+	+									+
−2	+	+	+	+									[+]	[+]	[+]	[+]	[+]	

Howitt 1891), as ZS by Flierl (in Howitt 1891), and again as ZS and as FMBS by Berndt (1953). That is to say, all the specifications in the different reports coincide with that given by Elkin (cf. Appendix to this chapter). If these are the facts, one has to think that either (i) the term *tidnara* is actually applied to different lines in the first ascending and the first descending genealogical levels (*yenku* and *kanini* lines respectively), or (ii) the term applies to all positions corresponding to Ego's moiety and the first descending level. This second point is a mere assumption based on the fact that at Ego's level the positions belonging to the *yenku* line are denoted by the term *yenku*, with the addition of *kaku* (eZ) and *niyi* (eB). As all the positions belonging to Ego's terminological division and genealogical level are distinguished by the

[10] As we saw, Howitt says that MMM (*kaia-kaia*) was generally addressed as *ngandri*, M, because she was the mother of a *kanini*.

terms *kaku* and *niyi*, it seems plausible that the children of the persons belonging to these categories (categories of Ego's moiety) are all categorized as *tidnara* (ZS, ZD).

On this assumption, the term *taru* (SW, DH) in the same genealogical level (first descending level), would denote an actual affinal status, as it certainly does in the first ascending genealogical level (WF, WFZ). But, taking into account these considerations it would not be easy to understand how the Dieri reckoned between marriageable and non-marriageable categories for the people classified in their own terminological division at that level. After all, they were concerned with the betrothal of people of that first descending level (the children of their sisters).

A second assumption is possible, and it refers to the distinction of the supposed *tidnara* of the first descending genealogical level according to whether they were the children of a *kaku* or of a *kaku-yenku*. They were concerned with the betrothal of the *tidnara* children of a *kaku*. The potential spouses of their children would then have been the *tidnara* children of their *kaku-yenku*.

In the same genealogical level, there is no problem with the term *ngatamura* (12), the specifications of which are S and D, and which is applied to the alternate positions in the first ascending and the first descending genealogical levels.

But the remaining terms, *paiera* (ZDH) and *kalari* (ZSW), introduce more problems. *Paiera* (11) is applied in the first ascending genealogical level to the actual mother of Ego's wife. It therefore denotes the mother of a *nadada*, the Ego's actual *noa*. But it is also applied to the brother of Ego's wife's mother. In the first descending genealogical level it is applied (as in the case of *tidnara*) to a position that belongs to another line. But the change of line can be explained by the change of line of the term *tidnara*. In the first ascending genealogical level, a *paiera* man is the actual husband of a *tidnara*. In the first descending genealogical level, *paiera* are again the actual husbands of some of Ego's *tidnara* (ZD). On the other hand, Ego is in the same relation to the *paiera* of the first ascending genealogical level as the mother's brother of Ego's wife, and Ego is the mother's brother of the wife of the *paiera* in the first descending genealogical level. Considering the rules of betrothal among the Dieri, the *paiera* of the first ascending genealogical level is involved in Ego's betrothal, as Ego is involved in the betrothal of the *paiera* in the first descending genealogical level. *Paiera* could then be a reciprocal term for all these positions related by the betrothal of the sister's children.

The term *kalari*, ZSW (18), is uniquely applied to one position in the first descending genealogical level of the *kami* line. It is, together with *ngaperi*, F (5), *ngandri*, M (6), *kaka*, MB (8), and *papa*, FZ (7), one of the small set of terms each of which is applied to only one position. The problems to explain with regard to this term relate to line and level: (i) why there is a distinct term in the *kami* line to denote this position, instead of a repetition of the term *papa*; and (ii) why there is a distinction by sex between *paiera* and *kalari* (ZDH and ZSW respectively) if this distinction does not apply to any other pair of positions at this genealogical level. Looking at Howitt's and Elkin's definitions of the term *kalari*, one finds that they give two different specifications: Elkin defines *kalari* as ZSW (m.s., by the convention of the diagram), but Howitt specifies the term as SW (w.s.). Considering that *paiera* is a reciprocal term, so that Ego is *paiera* to his ZSW and to his ZSH, and his ZDH is *paiera* to him, it seems that the logical term for the position of ZSW should be *paiera* also. The ethnography provides no means of resolving this issue.

IX

Going back now to the 'similarities' and 'disparities' pointed out by Lévi-Strauss between the Dieri system and an 'Aranda terminology', it is possible to see that the features signalized as common to both systems, namely:

(5) reciprocal terms between members of the second ascending and the second descending genealogical levels; and

(6) FFZ and MFZ classified with FMBW and MMBW respectively,

are two of the basic traits of a four-line symmetric prescriptive terminology. On the other hand, the dissimilarities between the two systems which Lévi-Strauss indicated, namely:

(7) cross-cousins are classified with FM and FMB (*kami*); and

(8) MMB ≠ MMBSS,

are basic features of a terminology of that kind based on matrilines.

There still remains the consideration of the number of terms. Lévi-Strauss says that the Dieri have only sixteen terms and 'this has no correlation whatsoever with the Aranda terminology or with the Kariera terminology or with the figure which might be calculated, on the basis of these two last, for a simple moiety system' (Lévi-Strauss 1949: 256). When considering the logic of a diagram representing a four-line symmetric prescriptive terminology we showed that a terminology consistent with that diagram could have even fewer than sixteen terms. In the analysis, we were also able to see that the number of terms of any terminology does not depend only on the distinctions that make it possible to define the terminology according to a diagram (cf. Needham 1963:228), but also on distinctions that refer to other levels of analysis. In the type we are describing, the diagnostic features are given by the distinction of four lines and the identifications in alternate genealogical levels. Distinctions according to sex are irrelevant to the formal definition of the type, and empirically (in this case) they occur in the first ascending and the first descending levels (on the assumption that Elkin's specification of *kalari*, ZSW, is correct), and they can be related to facts and rules belonging to other spheres of social organization.

There is no specific number of terms related to a specific type of terminology, as there are no specific social forms necessarily related to the different types of social classification. Concerning the number of terms, one could indicate what is the minimum for a certain definite type. Concerning social forms, such as moieties, sections and subsections, or types of local groups, one can only indicate whether they exist or not in a particular society, and, when they do, whether they are consistent or not with the classification provided by the relationship terminology.

If the Dieri had a system of social behaviour consistent with their relationship terminology (and the evidence demonstrates that they had), this would show that such a system does not necessarily imply subsections. The Dieri could distinguish individuals categorically, and not by their membership of actual institutions such as subsections.

A terminology can be classified, therefore, by its formal features. One can establish systems of social action consistent with a particular mode of social classification and prove empirically whether or not there is correspondence between both spheres.[11]

[11] An example of this type of analysis, correlating different types of relationship terminologies with their concomitant systems of actual behaviour regarding marriage, is presented in Needham's articles 'Terminology and Alliance, I: Garo, Manggarai' (1966), and 'Terminology and Alliance, II: Mapuche, Conclusions' (1967).

Considering the terminology from a formal point of view, the diagram to which one relates a set of terms is a consequence of the application of certain basic principles. We call 'basic principles' the criteria by which categories are distinguished, and these criteria could be genetically related to certain basic forms of empirical organization and the transmission of rights from one generation to another.

Lévi-Strauss's idea of relating systems of 'restricted exchange' to 'disharmonic regimes' is, as we have already seen in chapter 2, a reformulation of the explanation Durkheim gives for section systems. For Durkheim, a section system is a result of patrilocal residence and matrilineal descent (Durkheim 1898: 18-19). For Lévi-Strauss, patrilocality and matriliny are the indicators of 'restricted exchange' (Lévi-Strauss 1949: 271). The difference between the two hypotheses lies in the fact that, while one is an explanatory hypothesis concerning a particular type, the second proposes an empirical correspondence between systems and regimes. Durkheim relates the existence of four-section systems to the separation of adjacent generations within a single local group, because adjacent generations in a patrilocal group belong to different matrilineal moieties, but living together they are 'too near' each other to be allowed to intermarry.[12]

Following Durkheim's idea, a four-line symmetric prescriptive terminology could respond to the separation of people belonging to opposite lines but living in the same local group. If the Dieri were divided into exogamous matrilineal moieties and residence was patrilocal, in order to avoid marriage with people who were 'too near' their own line (or their own matrilineal totem) because they lived in the same local group with individuals of their own line (as in the case of *kaka*'s children, MBC), they could devise another line in the opposite moiety. In this way, individuals from a single line and consecutive genealogical levels would marry in different lines of the opposite moiety. That is to say, they married in the line where their mothers and mother's brothers did not marry and in a different local group. This fact accounts for the

---

[12] While Durkheim's hypothesis applies in the case of a four-section system with matrilineal moieties and patrilocal residence, or in the case of the Dieri (matrilines, matrilineal moieties, and patrilocal residence), it does not apply, for obvious reasons, to the explanation of a four-section system, an eight-subsection system, or a four-line terminology with patrilines, patrilineal moieties, and patrilocal residence. See chapter 2 above and chapter 6 below.

identifications in alternate genealogical levels and for the pre-scribed category. The resulting system might be considered as the result of the concurrence of a matrilineal principle and the creating of 'implicit patrilineal moieties' (Lane and Lane 1962: 50), but the only principle that seems to be applied in Dieri society is a matrilineal principle in a patrilocal society. What the Dieri people perhaps had in mind was not to marry a *kami* because their *kami* lived in the same local group of the people of their own exogamous totemic group and their own line, and this was probably the cause of distinguishing another line in the opposite moiety.

Why then recognize another line in their own moiety? Pre-sumably because their own children belonged to the opposite moiety and therefore married in Ego's moiety, within which concordant distinctions needed to be made.

For the sake of clarity we have given a hypothetical genetic evolution of a four-matriline symmetric prescriptive terminology, assuming the existence of actual exogamous moieties. We have proceeded in this way because the Dieri terminology is our example and the Dieri actually possessed exogamous matrilineal moieties. But the same reasoning could be followed starting with a hypothetical case of a two-line symmetric prescriptive terminology based on matrilines in a society with patrilocal residence. Only in the case of a mode of classification such as that of the Dieri, the concomitant system of actual behaviour is complicated enough to make us think that they had to make use of definite social institu-tions (in this case exogamous moieties) in order to make it simpler. If our assumption is correct, it can then be imagined that the Dieri might have created eight subsections in order to reinforce their mode of classification; but, if so, they certainly would not have needed to start with the creation of four sections.

Our point is that one does not need to think that because a 'four-section' system has four sections and an 'eight-section' system has eight subsections, and because 8 is a multiple of 4, there is therefore 'a genetic relation between eight-section and four-section systems' (Lévi-Strauss 1962a: 74). If, however, one is 'tempted' to interpret moiety, section, and subsection systems according to the 'natural "order": 2, 4, 8' (Lévi-Strauss 1962d: 54), one is bound to consider the Dieri system as a case of 'apparent form of eight-section *structure*' (Lévi-Strauss 1949: 275), and to give as a possible evolution of the system the change from 'generalized exchange' to 'restricted exchange' (Lévi-Strauss 1949: 275).

How to justify such a hypothesis if the Dieri relationship terminology is one of the neatest examples of a four-line symmetric prescriptive terminology, and if the genetic principles for such a mode of social classification are seen as the concurrence of matrilineal descent and patrilocal residence?

The justification lies, for Lévi-Strauss, in a diagram which does not correspond to the Dieri relationship terminology (cf. Lévi-strauss 1949: 260, Figure 40).[13] Lévi-Strauss understands the Dieri relationship terminology to be based on four patrilines and the diagram he presents corresponds to this conception. He then asks 'whence does the dichotomy preventing the marriage of cross-cousins arise?'[14] because it seems to be 'a sort of needless elaboration', and 'how it is that the four terms *yenku*, *nadada*, *kami* and *ngatamura* circulate through several lines?' (Lévi-Strauss 1949: 257). Posed in this way the questions are not easy to answer, and Lévi-Strauss demonstrates this by giving the possible evolution of the system as 'firstly, an archaic system with four matrilineal and matrilocal lines based on generalized exchange . . . ; secondly, the adaptation to a Mara–Anula system; and, finally, the present system' (Lévi-Strauss 1949: 262). He adds, moreover, that even if this is a purely hypothetical sequence, it is 'the only one allowing the anomalies of the system to be understood'.

Looking at the Dieri relationship terminology as based on matrilines, however, it is clear that the terms *yenku*, *nadada*, *kami*, and *ngatamura* do not at all 'circulate through several lines' but that they are systematically applied to alternate genealogical levels, each within a single line. We hope we have demonstrated that there are no such anomalies to be understood.[15]

---

[13] Figure 40 in the English edition of *Les Structures élémentaires de la parenté* (p. 206) lacks the lines connecting the outer masculine positions, though its constitution is none the less clear.

[14] cf. n. 6 above.

[15] After this monograph had been submitted for publication, I learned of certain earlier references to the Dieri, by H. K. Fry, that accord well with my analysis and which I should like to acknowledge. (They are not listed under 'Dieri' in Greenway's bibliography [p. 413], and Lévi-Strauss does not mention them.)

Fry cites the Dieri as an example of a society with 'maternal descent' and moieties only, i.e. with no named subsections, yet as having 'an eight-class organisation' (1931: 13). A later paper contains interesting comments on the

Lévi-Strauss's interpretation seems to be based on his belief in a genetic connection between 'four-section' and 'eight-section' systems, and on the consideration of systems with an 'Aranda rule' but without subsections as anomalous and deriving from 'generalized exchange'. Our analysis, by contrast, is based on the formal analysis of relationship terminologies, and on the discrimination of two kinds of symmetric prescriptive terminologies: those based on two lines and those based on four (whether patrilines or matrilines). 'Four-section' systems would thence be considered as systems possessing a two-line symmetric terminology (see Needham 1966: 142 n. 2), and the possible explanation for the existence of the four sections accounts also for the existence of symmetric prescriptive terminologies based on four matrilines.

---

terms *nadada* and *kami* (1934: 16). In 1934, moreover, he himself was given 'numerous kinship terms' by an old Dieri man, and was convinced by a subsequent check that most of these were correct. In what appears to have been his latest reference to this society, in the course of making a contrast between patrilineal Aranda and matrilineal Dieri usages, he further elaborates on *nadada* and *kami* and also presents a diagram of eight matrilineal 'subclass divisions' (1950: 290).

While gladly recognizing Mr Fry's priority in arriving in these respects at a basically correct characterization of Dieri society, I trust I may observe nevertheless that his brief allusions to this system are incidental examples in more general arguments, and that they do not supply an intensive demonstration such as I have worked out above. It is a point of theoretical consequence, also, that his preponderant and constant concern, in a series of statements, is to prove that 'the marriage system customary in a tribe of eight subclass divisions was also customary in the great majority of Australian tribes, both patrilineal and matrilineal, and whether named class divisions or moieties were recognized or not' (1957: 2; cf. 1934: 20; 1950: 283-4).

Chapter Five

A Question of Preferences: the Iatmül Case

I

Lévi-Strauss states that 'an elementary structure can be equally preferential or prescriptive':

> neither prescription nor preference is the test of an elementary structure. Its one and only criterion rests in the fact that, preferred or prescribed, the spouse is the spouse solely because she belongs to an alliance category or stands in a certain kinship relationship to Ego. In other words, the imperative or desirable relationship is a function of the social structure (1967: xxi-xxii).

According to this, it should be possible to categorize a system with preferential marriage into one or another type of elementary structure.

In relation to this problem we have chosen to analyse here the Iatmül system of alliances and the Iatmül relationship terminology because, according to Bateson, 'not only have they three positive marriage rules which conflict one with another . . . but the people do not adhere even to their negative rules' (Bateson 1936: 91).

The question whether this system should hence be classified, according to Lévi-Strauss's typology, as a 'complex structure' is ruled out, because for Lévi-Strauss 'complex structures' are those 'systems which limit themselves to defining the circle of relatives and leave the determination of the spouse to other mechanisms economic or psychological' (1949: ix). On the other hand, since for Lévi-Strauss a preferential rule has the same analytical value as a prescription, and the Iatmül do have declared 'preferences', the system has to be considered in Lévi-Strauss's own scheme as an 'elementary structure'.

The purposes of our analysis are twofold: (1) to classify the

Iatmül relationship terminology and relate it to the actual system of alliances, and (2) to determine once more, but this time in the light of an empirical example, the consistency and applicability of Lévi-Strauss's definitions of 'prescription', 'preference', 'elementary structure', and 'complex structure'.[1]

II

There are four reports of Iatmül society in the form of three articles (Bateson 1932a, 1932b, 1935) and a monograph (Bateson 1936).[2]

The articles of 1932 were published by Bateson after his first contact, lasting six months, with Iatmül society. His admirable book *Naven* (1936) was published after he completed his fieldwork in the area with a second sojourn, extending to an additional fifteen months, among the Iatmül people: it consists mainly of the description of the *naven* ceremony among them.[3]

[1] I am obliged to Mr Bateson for a note of confirmation (July 1969) about the published sources on the Iatmül.
   Mr Anthony Forge has very kindly composed a commentary on the analysis presented here: 'Marriage and Exchange in the Sepik'. It forms chapter 6 of ASA Monograph 11, *Rethinking Kinship and Marriage*, ed. R. Needham (1971a).
[2] Hereafter, references to Bateson's ethnographic accounts of the Iatmül will be made by year and page only.
[3] Bateson's book (1936) was reviewed by Nadel (1937), Elkin (1938), and Powder-maker (1940).

Murdock has analysed the Iatmül system in *Social Structure* (1949). He characterizes the system as patrilineal and patrilocal. He correctly records 'patri-moieties', but is mistaken in stating that these are exogamous, for Bateson expressly says that 'none of these groups [viz. moieties, phratries, clans] are strictly exogamous' (1936: 4). Murdock further states of the Iatmül that clans are 'unreported', whereas Bateson repeatedly refers to patrilineal clans (1932a: 257; 1936: 52, 310). The relationship terminology, finally, is typed as 'Omaha', i.e. as characterized by the features FZD = ZD and/or MBD = MZ (Murdock 1949: 224), whereas in fact, as will be set out below, although the Iatmül terminology includes MBD = MZ, it definitely distinguishes FZD ≠ ZD.

Peter Lucich, in *The Development of Omaha Kinship Terminologies in three Australian Aboriginal Tribes of the Kimberley Division, Western Australia* (1968), also ascribes 'Omaha features' to the Iatmül terminology. He does not analyse the system, but mentions that the Iatmül have patrimoieties, 'prescribed marriage with a consanguineal relative from the FM's descent group', and also 'two-generational alternation of personal names consistent with a four-section system' (p. 249). That the Iatmül have an alternation of personal names is certainly true, but one could hardly say that this alternation is consistent with a four-section system, except for the irrelevant fact that the sections alternate by genealogical level (cf. chapter 6).

D. M. Schneider, in 'Some Muddles in the Models' (1965: 25-80), mentions

G

When Bateson refers to the Iatmül, he denotes a population living in a number of villages on the banks of the Sepik River in New Guinea. He calls Iatmül the part of the linguistic group (100 miles in length) that recognize themselves as a unit (1932a: 249). 'Iatmül' is, in fact, the name of a very small clan of one of the villages (Mindimbit), and the compound term Iatmül-iambonai[4] is used by the people of Mindimbit to denote the whole linguistic group.

Three divisions are distinguished: Eastern, Central, and Western Iatmül (1936: 142, 228 n. 1, 239), which vary apparently in culture and in definiteness of organization. Bateson found the culture in this area sufficiently uniform for his purpose: 'there are, however, local variations of many kinds, not confined to superficial details, but definite modifications of kinship system, clan system, and the scheme of ceremonial life' (1932b: 450).

The Iatmül are characterized by Bateson as a 'fine, proud, head-hunting people' (1936: 4) who depend almost entirely on the river and the fens for their food and life. Although they work sago for themselves, they also trade fish for sago produced by the 'bush people' (1936: 7, 234); trading rights with bush villages are recognized and jealously guarded (1932b: 283). All communication with other Iatmül villages is done by canoe (except in the very dry season), which is also the way of travelling for any other purposes such as trading, fishing, or head-hunting.

There is no centralized organization and the separate villages are independent war-making groups, though a pair of villages may unite in a feud against another. They are independent units for ceremonial purposes also, though a great many natives go to see and to take part in dances in neighbouring villages. There is no hereditary rank or chieftainship.

---

the Iatmül as one of the cases that 'seem fit to' (*sc.* 'seem to fit'?) the models of 'patrilateral prescriptive systems . . . provided there is no insistence on the kind of perfection in their concrete manifestation which Needham demands' (p. 71). He does not, however, analyse the system, nor does he refer to any demonstration of the cogency of his assertion.

Finally, Lorenz G. Löffler, in 'Symmetrische und Asymmetrische Allianz-systeme' (1967), makes a reference to an analysis of Bateson's data, by W. Brüggemann, which has not yet appeared in print.

[4] *Iambon* is an adjective referring to the 'Upper River' and is applied equally to those who speak variants of the same language and to foreigners higher up the river (Bateson 1932a: 249 n. 2).

There is not in Bateson's works any indication of the total population of Iatmül society. Nor is there any indication of the number of villages. Some of them are: Mindimbit, Palimbai, Tambunum, Malingei, Kankanamun (1932a, 1936). He states that the average population of each village varies between 200 and 1000 individuals.

The villages are divided into two patrilineal totemic moieties and two patrilineal ceremonial moieties. The totemic moieties are subdivided into patrilineal clans (*ngaiva*): there are between fifty and a hundred clans of which between ten or twenty are represented in any one village (1936: 307). The village of Mindimbit contained 'representatives' of eight clans (1932b: 402). The clans are paired and trace descent from a pair of brothers, one clan being called the 'elder brother' of the other. 'Larger groups of clans also occur' (1936: 310). There is also a grouping called *nggwoil-nggu*, composed of 'a close patrilineal group within the clan' (1936: 104 n. 2).

There is in some villages (Bateson describes Malingei as the most perfect of them) a complete correspondence between the division into patrilineal totemic moieties and patrilineal clans and the physical organization. Malingei is divided longitudinally by a big dancing-ground (*wonpunau*) on which the ceremonial houses stand. On one side of this area are the houses of one patrilineal moiety and on the other side the houses of the opposite moiety.

The names of the totemic moieties and their functional importance concerning initiation vary from the Eastern Iatmül (Mindimbit, etc.) to Central Iatmül (Kankanamun, etc.). Among the latter, both the initiatory moieties and the totemic moieties are called 'Sun' and 'Mother', in spite of the fact that several clans which belong totemically to one moiety have gone across to the other moieties for initiatory purposes. But, in Mindimbit, the initiatory dual division is regarded as entirely distinct from the totemic moieties, and the initiatory moieties are not called 'Sun' and 'Mother', but Kiship and Miwot (1936: 228 n.).

A father has authority over his son, and an elder brother over a younger brother (1936: 98). Inheritance is patrilineal (1936: 211), and brothers are 'expected to quarrel over their patrimony' (1936: 212).

When Bateson worked among the Iatmül, the villages contained 'considerable numbers' of young people who had recently returned to their homes after spending from three to five years as indentured labourers on European plantations and in gold-mines (1936: 167). During his stay in Mindimbit, where he did all his work on his first expedition, 'all the available young men had left the village to work for Europeans' (1932a: 275). His account makes a number of references to a marked degree of cultural change brought about both by these influences and by the British administration. A village constable and a government interpreter were permanently stationed in Mindimbit (1932a: 266, 282). Missionaries, too, worked to disintegrate Iatmül culture. At some villages, they even lined up the women and got mission-trained men to perform on the sacred flutes in front of them – a gross and irreparable exposure of a 'mystery upon which the separation of the sexes is based' (1935: 163, 170). In Mindimbit the initiation system had broken down, the rising generations were in a 'lawless state', and the older men were 'fatalist before the decay of their culture' (1932a: 274-5). Bateson speaks indeed of a 'dying culture' (1932b: 440).

According to Bateson, 'neither of the systems of dual divisions controls marriage in a simple way', and there is a definite preference for clan exogamy (1932a: 257). Marriage is patrilocal (1936: 52), the wife going to live in the husband's *ngaiva*. This word has a definite local reference as well as meaning clan, and a clan can be referred to as 'part of the village' (1932b: 401).

A man has authority over his wife (1936: 98 n. 1); novices in initiation ceremonies, who are 'mercilessly bullied', are known as 'wives' (131). Wife-takers are inferior to wife-givers (1936: 79).

The totemic patrilineal clans are divided in *mbapma* (the literal translation of which is 'line') which contain members of the clan belonging to alternate generations. Thus, FF, Ego, and SS form a *mbapma*, while F and S form another *mbapma* of the same clan. The correspondence of generations in different clans, Bateson says (1932a: 269), can be traced by reference to the system of totemic names and by comparing the terms used by different persons in addressing the shamanic spirit. The Iatmül have a complicated system of personal names. Every individual bears names of totemic ancestors, viz. spirits, birds, stars, animals, pots, adzes, etc. An individual may have hundreds of these names which refer in their etymology to secret myths (1936: 127).

Regarding the *mbapma* system, Bateson adds that this system 'does not control marriage', and so the kinship terms used towards women are independent of *mbapma* (1932a: 269).

III

The relationship terminology is as in *Table 7*. The range of

Table 7

*Iatmül Relationship Terminology**

1.	*nggwail*	FF, FFZ, SS, SD†
2.	*nyamun*	FF, eB, B (w.s.), eZ (w.s.)
3.	*iai*	FM, FMBS, FMBD, FMBSD, all women of the same clan as these
4.	*tagwa*	FM, W; woman
5.	*mbuambo*	MF, MM, MBS, MBD, MBSW, FeB, MBSSS
6.	*nyanggai*	FFZ, Z, SD
7.	*tawontu*	FMB, WB, FMBS, FMBSW, FMBSS, FMBSSW, WBSS
8.	*nyai'*	F, FB
9.	*nyame*	M, MZ, MBD, SW (w.s.), MBSD, MBSSD
10.	*iau*	FZ
11.	*wau*	MB, MMZS, MBSS, SWB
12.	*nondu*	FZH, DH, HZH
13.	*mbora*	MBW, MBSSW, SWBW
14.	*naisagut*	WF, WM, WMB, FMBW, WBW, FMBS, FMBSW, WBC
15.	*laua*	ZHF, ZC, Z (widowed)
16.	*tshuambo*	yB, HyB, SS (m.s.), yZ (w.s.)
17.	*tshaishi*	eBW‡
18.	*lan*	H
19.	*lando*	ZH, ZHB, ZSS; men who might marry Ego's sister
20.	*nian*	S, D, BC, FZC (w.s.)
21.	*kauggat*	BC (w.s.)
22.	*na*	FZC, MMZS, DC
23.	*ianan*	FZSS, ZSS, SS (w.s.)
24.	*kaishe-ragwa*	ZSW
25.	*nasa*	HZC

* From Bateson 1932a: 263-70; 1936: 16, 18, 50, 93, 243, 305-12. The terms displayed in Bateson's diagram (1936: 305) have been augmented by details taken from the text. For this and other reasons the numbering does not always accord with that in his diagram.
† There is also a term, *warangka*, the specification of which is FFF. The term also means 'patrilineal ancestor'.
‡ Bateson's diagram (1936: 305) incorrectly has *tshaishi*, Z; *nyamun*, ZH.

application of the terminology is not reported, but Bateson makes it clear that:

> by his genealogy at birth a man is provided with a series of relatives – not only real brothers and sisters, parents, uncles, etc., but also with a complete set of relatives-in-law and potential wives. According to this system of reckoning, a man's possible wives are the women of his father's mother's clan (1932a: 263).

These women are termed Ego's *iai*. Their clan is referred to by Ego as *iai nampa*, father's mother people (*nampa*, people), or as *towa-naisagut*, a collective term for the members of wife's clan (1932a: 263; 1936: 311).

The terms for the other related clans – that are 'in constant use' (1932a: 268) – are *wau-nyame nampa*, mother's brother and mother people, *laua nyanggu*,[5] sister's child people, and *lanoa nampa*, husband people. Ego's own clan is referred as *nggwail warangka*, a collective term meaning 'patrilineal ancestors' (*nggwail*, FF; *warangka*, FFF). The clan where Ego's daughter marries is called *kaishe nampa*.

The use of the kinship terms, says Bateson, may be related by the Iatmül not to genealogy but to the system of patrilineal clans (*ngaiva*) (1932a: 268).

IV

There are three explicit and conflicting rules of marriage:

1 Marriage with *iai* (FMBSD; in general, women of FM clan). This rule is expressed in statements such as 'a woman should climb the same ladder that her father's father's sister climbed' (1936: 88).[6] After marriage, this *iai* is called *tagwa* or *iairagwa* (woman, wife, FFW). Such a rule can be represented in a diagram as in *Figure 15*:

2 Marriage with *na* (FZD). This rule is expressed in sayings such as: 'the daughter goes in payment for the mother' (1936: 89). A rule of this kind is to be represented as a patrilateral asymmetric system such as in *Figure 16*.

---

[5] *Nampa* (people) and *nyanggu* (children) are used as synonyms (Bateson 1936: 310).

[6] Bateson refers to this rule as being expressed as such in Kankanumun (1936: 89 n. 1).

Concerning rules (1) and (2), Bateson remarks that these two rules, although contradictory, are connected in a 'curious way' (1936: 89). He refers to the fact that in a system of FZD marriage the category that contains the specification FZD also contains the

Figure 15 Marriage with *iai* (FMBSD)   *Figure 16* Marriage with *na* (FZD)

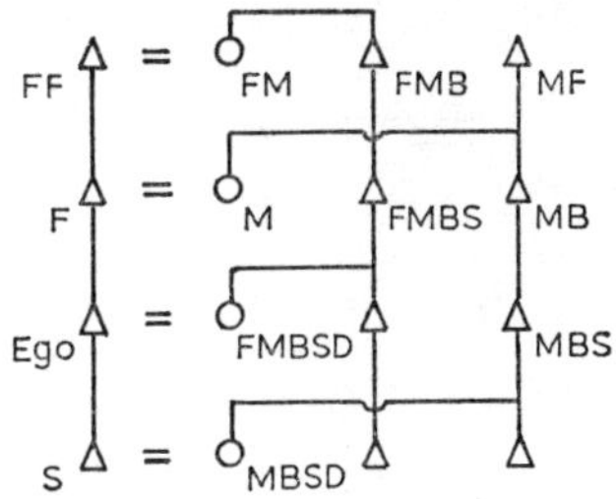

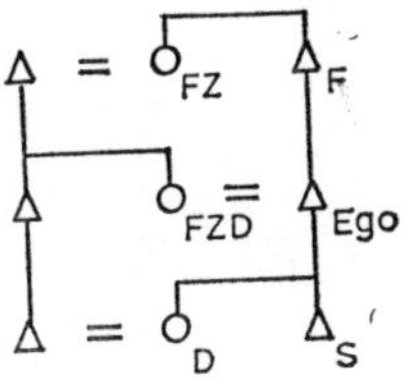

specification FMBSD. This situation he displays as in *Figure 17 (a)*, which may more clearly be reconstructed as in *Figure 17 (b)*.

A curiosity of another kind is that 'in certain cases, when the offspring of the marriage are male instead of female, one of the sons will be sent, while still a baby, for *adoption* into the family and clan of the man who gave his sister to the father for wife, i.e.

Figure 17 FZD = FMBSD marriage

Figure 17a (Bateson 1936: 89)   *Figure 17b*

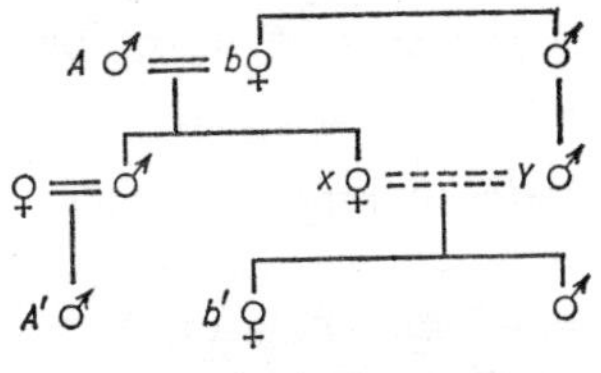

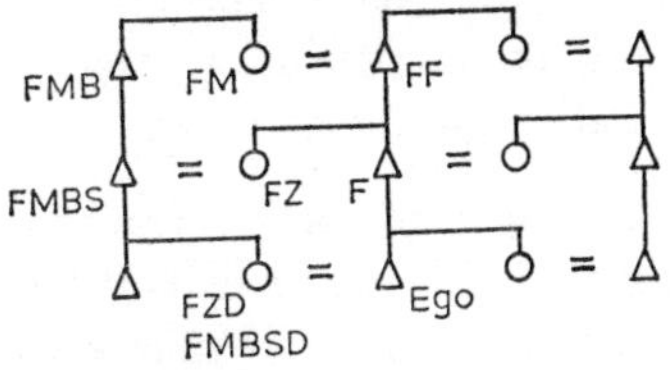

the boy is adopted by his mother's brother, to whom he goes in payment for his mother' (1936: 89 n. 2). Bateson himself met a man who had in fact been adopted and brought up by his mother's brother (1932a: 266), perhaps under this arrangement. This situation is represented in *Figure 18*.

3 Exchange of sisters (*Figure 19*). This rule is expressed as 'women should be exchanged' (1936: 90). Bateson notes that this

rule, although contradictory with both rule (1) and rule (2), applies not only to sister exchange but to FZD marriage (rule 2). This type of marriage is referred to by Bateson in his first paper (1932a: 264-5) as deriving from the *tambinien* relationship. *Tambinien* are partners from opposite moieties whose children ought to marry with brother–sister exchange.

Figure 18 Adoption of ZS   *Figure 19* Sister exchange

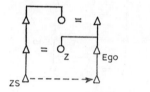

Concerning these three rules (1, 2, and 3), Bateson says:

it is quite likely that the marriage with father's sister's daughter has been evolved in the culture through interaction of the two systems, *iai* marriage and sister exchange. The whole kinship vocabulary would point to the *iai* system as the older, and the concept of exchange of women may well have been adopted from neighbouring peoples. In this connection it is interesting that one of the young men whom I used as an informant had a strong impression that the correct term for father's sister's daughter was *iai*. But after we had discussed the matter in detail, he was uncertain and consulted one of the older men who stated definitely that *na* was the correct term for this relative (1936: 90 n. 1).

In a note to page 89 of *Naven*, Bateson refers, in fact, to a fourth 'cliché', as he calls it:

4 '*Laua*'s son will marry *wau*'s daughter.' Bateson says that this is another way of referring to *iai* marriage, but the *iai* specified as FMBD.[7]

The difference from rule (1), also referring to *iai* marriage, is that while the latter expresses a rule concerning people of the same genealogical level, this new one (FMBD marriage) relates people of two consecutive genealogical levels, as it is shown in *Figure 20*.

[7] This rule was collected in Mindimbit and Palimbai (1936: 89 n. 1).

There is in addition a kind of 'extension of the affinal system'. This is the relationship between 'certain pairs of clans which regard each other reciprocally as *lanoa nampa* or *laua nyanggu* –

Figure 20 FMBD marriage (*wau*'s daughter/*laua*'s son marriage)

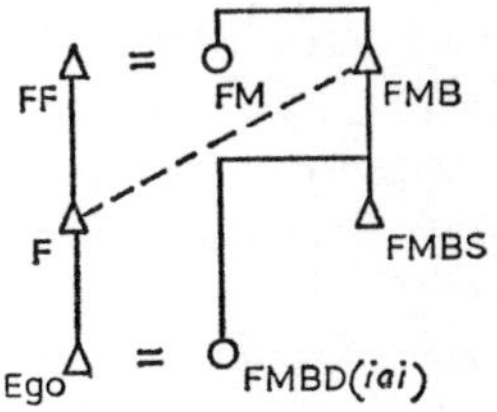

FF = FM — FMB

F — FMBS

Note: - - - - - = *wau*/*laua* relationship Ego = FMBD(*iai*)

both terms are used . . . .This relationship is reciprocal between clans and apparently rests not upon any particular past or present marriage, but upon a tradition that the women of one clan often marry the men of the other and *vice-versa*. . . . This clan relationship is practically without effect outside the ceremonial houses' (1936: 96 n. 2).

V

Iatmül men can have several wives. They may come from a number of clans, as many as eight or ten (1932a: 286-7). Among these, Bateson believes that the *iai* wife (*tagwa, iairagwa*) should be treated quite differently from the wives acquired in other ways (1932a: 280). The *iai* wife is not 'bought', whereas others may be (1932a: 280). A man's *iai* may enter his house and become his wife of her own volition, and he cannot refuse. He cannot divorce this wife, either, and there is a definite avoidance of her name. But, although there is always among the wives of a man one who is more influential than the others (*nemwan tagwa*),[8] this one is not necessarily the *iai* wife (1932a: 287).

VI

Regarding negative rules, Bateson says that they are 'very vague' (1936: 91). There is a strong feeling against marrying one's own sister, and he never knew of any case of this sort. The next strongest ban is that upon marriage with any of the relatives called *naisagut* (WM, WBD). 'A man must never marry his wife's

[8] The word *nemwan* means 'big, great' (1936: 310).

brother's wife' (1932a: 288), i.e. a woman of the category *naisagut.* 'Such marriages are rare,' he says, 'but when we turn to the less stringent prohibitions, as of marriage with classificatory "sisters", women of own clan with whom genealogical connections can easily be traced, we find that such women are sometimes taken as wives' (1936: 91), though it is said to be wrong (1932a: 288). The Iatmül even rather approve of these endogamous marriages and say that from endogamy are produced long and widely ramifying lines of descendants (1936: 91); and in fact the solitary marriage of which Bateson provides a genealogical illustration is precisely of a man with his MMZSD (1936: 103) – which may be reduced to MBD – i.e. his *nyame*, 'mother'.

Besides these rules and types of marriage, there are many marriages with outside groups, e.g. with women captured in war, or sent as peace offerings, women met in trading expeditions, etc. These women, however, occupy a segregated status, for they are 'foreigners' whose heads can be taken. One man met by Bateson even wore headhunter's insigna for the killing of his wife, who had come from another village (1936: 139). It needs 'extraordinary courage' for a woman to go alone to a 'foreign village' (145).

To sum up the marriage system, Bateson says that, in practice, 'marriage occurs very nearly at random' (1936: 92). But this randomness does not seem to be an ideal for the Iatmül, nor do they seem to recognize it as a trait of their own behaviour. When talking about their neighbours they refer to them as 'dogs and pigs who mate at random' (1936: 91).[9]

VII

Before trying to assess what kind of 'elementary structure' the different Iatmül preferences fit, let us analyse the formal traits of the Iatmül relationship terminology.

Bateson's diagram of the Iatmül relationship terminology (1936: 305; my *Figure 21*) divides it into consanguineal and affinal terms. His diagram of affinal terms is not complete,[10] and this is probably due to the fact that in the Iatmül relationship terminology the majority of the terms have both consanguineal and affinal

---

[9] Bateson does not quote the Iatmül phrase or provide any gloss on the Iatmül equivalent of this statistical concept.

[10] There are no affinal terms given for Ego's children or grandchildren positions.

Figure 21 Bateson's diagram of the Iatmül relationship terminology
(1936: 305)

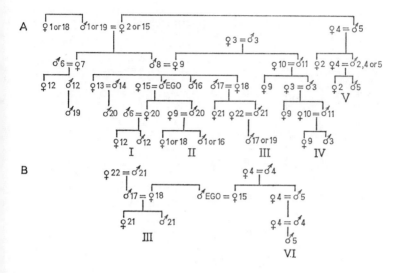

Note: The diagram incorrectly has *tshaishi* (13), Z; *nyamun* (14), ZH.

A, Consanguineous terms (m.s.). B, Affinal terms (m.s.).
♂, male. ♀, female. =, marriage. |, descent. ⌐——¬, siblingship.

Arabic numbers refer to terms for individuals. Roman numbers refer to
terms for patrilineal groups seen collectively.

1. *nggwail*.	7. *iau*.	13. *tshaishi*.	19. *ianan*.
2. *iai*.	8. *nyai'*.	14. *nyamun*.	20. *nian*.
3. *mbuambo*.	9. *nyame*.	15. *tagwa*.	21. *laua*.
4. *naisagut*.	10. *mbora*.	16. *tshuambo*.	22. *kaisheragwa*.
5. *tawonto*.	11. *wau*.	17. *lando*.	
6. *nondu*.	12. *na*.	18. *nyanggai*.	

I. *kaishe-nampa*.
II. Own clan.
III. *lanoa-nampa* or *laua nyanggu*.
IV. *wau-nyame*. (Son's *iai nampa*.)

V. iai-nampa. (Become *towa-naisagut* if Ego marries one of their women.)
VI. *towa-naisagut*. (Son's *wau-nyame*.)

specifications, so that it is factitious to separate them into different diagrams.

Our own diagram of the Iatmül relationship terminology

Figure 22 The Itamül relationship terminology (cf. *Table 7*)

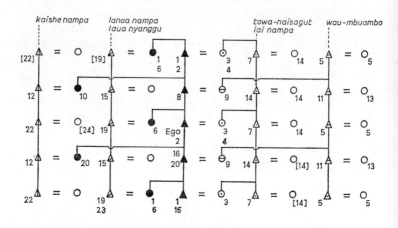

(*Figure 22*) contains all the terms provided by the ethnography (cf. *Table 7*), and is arranged according to the following traits:

1 *Linearity*. The equations and distinctions indicating linearity are:

    (i) F = FB
    (ii) F = MZ
    (iii) FB ≠ MB
    (iv) FFB ≠ MFB
    (v) FFZ ≠ MFZ
    (vi) FM ≠ MM
    (vii) FZC ≠ MZC
    (viii) FBC ≠ MBC
    (ix) ZC ≠ BC ≠ WBC

2 *Cycles*. There are two kinds of cycle, exhibited in alternate genealogical levels:

    (i) direct, connecting adjacent descent lines;
    (ii) indirect, connecting alternate descent lines.

3 *Asymmetry*. The distinctions indicating asymmetry are:

  (i) FFZ ≠ FMBW
 (ii) FZ ≠ MBW
(iii) Z ≠ WBW

4 *Alternation*. The equations indicating alternation of terms by genealogical levels are:

  (i) FF = SS; F = S
 (ii) FFZ = Z = SD
(iii) FFW = W
 (iv) MF = MFSS; MB = MBSS
  (v) FMB = FMBSS; FMBS = FMBSSS
 (vi) ZH = ZSS; ZHF = ZS
(vii) FZS = DS; ZHF = DH
(viii) MBW = MBSSW = SWBW
 (ix) MM = MBSW

VIII

For all male and female positions in Ego's line there is the indication of a prescribed category consistently defined as FMBSD (*iai*) for the male positions, and FFZSS (*lando*) for the female positions. Thus, there is a prescribed category (*iai*) specified as FMBSD whenever there is ethnographic evidence on the line to which the category specified as 'spouse' belongs.

There are in the terminology five patrilines headed by the terms *nggwail* (FF), *tawontu* (FMB), *mbuambo* (MF), *lando* (FFZH), and *nondu* (FZH). The patrilines coincide with a classification of those related clans which have special designations, viz. *nggwail warangka*, own clan; *towa-naisagut* or *iai nampa*, FMB and W clan; *wau-nyame nampa* (or *wau-mbuambo*), M and MB clan; *lanoa nampa* or *laua nyanggu*, ZH and ZC clan; and *kaishe nampa*, DH clan.

In Bateson's account, the terms *lanoa nampa*, 'a collective term for the members of the patrilineal group into which the speaker's sister has married', and *laua nyanggu*, 'the patrilineal group which includes the speaker's classificatory *lauas*', are given as if they could refer to different patrilineal groups (1936: 309). From the composition of the relationship terminology it is clear that the categories by which the people of both patrilineal groups are addressed belong to the same patriline. They would belong to the same patrilineal group as well if *iai* marriages alone were contracted, the line being composed of *lando*, FZHF, ZH, and DH, and *laua*, ZHF and ZS. But the existence of two designations for this set of categories probably derives from the fact that there are forms of marriage other than with the *iai*, so that one of the designations (*lanoa nampa*) is purely affinal for the group of relatives-in-law deriving from one of the sisters not married to a person categorized as *lando* (FFZSS).

The same probably applies to *iai nampa* and *towa-naisagut* (FMB and W clans). If a *iai* marriage is contracted by Ego, the categories *tawontu* (FMB, FMBSS, WB, and WBSS) and *naisagut* (WF, FMBS, and WBS) belong, together with *iai* (women of the FMB clan), to the same patrilineal group, just as they belong to the same patriline. But if Ego contracts marriages other than with the *iai*, the *towa-naisagut* (WF, WB) relatives he acquires are in a different patrilineal group from his *iai*.

Kaishe nampa is the patrilineal group into which Ego's daughter is supposed to marry. It coincides with the patriline composed by the terms *nondu* (FZH, DH) and *na* (ZC and DC) if Ego's daughter is actually married into the same patrilineal group where her FFZ was married. But here again there is an ambiguity, due probably to the same inconsistency in actual marriages. The designation for the whole group (*kaishe nampa*) derives from *kaishe ragwa* (child's spouse's mother) which should be specified then only as FZSW, viz. *na*'s wife and *nondu*'s mother. But Bateson adds to these specifications of *kaishe-ragwa* that 'sister's son's wife may be called *kaishe-ragwa*' (1936: 309). This specification corresponds to the line into which Ego's sister is married, and not to the one where Ego's father's sister is married. It could mean that both daughter's husband's mother and daughter's daughter's husband's mother are denoted by the same term, or that, again, marriages other than *iai* were contracted. In fact, the type of marriage that would coincide with the specification of *kaishe-ragwa* as ZSW, would be the '*laua*'s son–*wau*'s daughter' marriage, already seen as rule (4).

IX

Apart from *kaishe ragwa*, there is no other inconsistency in the Iatmül relationship terminology. The terms can be consistently arranged in an asymmetric prescriptive terminology composed of five patrilines and with alternation of terms by genealogical level (cf. *Figure 22*).

The ethnography provides data enough to arrange at least all positions in Ego's line according to this scheme. It does not provide, however, the necessary data for an understanding of the lines to which belong the categories specified as 'wives' of male positions of the other four lines not related affinally with Ego's line. This applies to *tawontu* and *naisagut* wives (FMBW, FMBSW, WBW), all designated as *naisagut*; *mbuambo* and *wau* wives (MM, MBW, MBSW, SWBW), designated as *mbuambo* (*mbuambo*'s wives) and *mbora* (*wau*'s wives); *laua*'s wives (ZHFW, ZSW), designated perhaps as *kaishe ragwa*.

Figure 23 Hypothetical asymmetric ('matrilateral') system

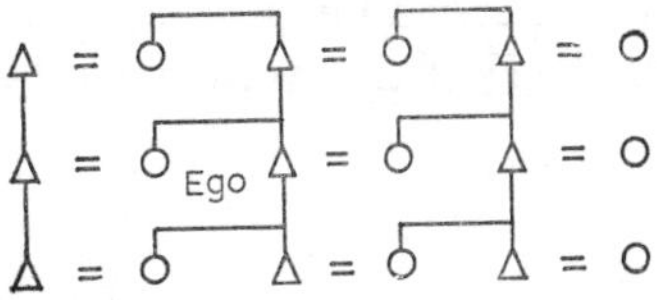

But still, even with this lack of information about some specifications, the connections of Ego's line with the other four constitute an asymmetric prescriptive terminology, only one that is incomplete. It would be a case similar to that of an asymmetric prescriptive terminology composed of three lines in which the categories reported by the ethnographer were disposed as in *Figure 23*. The specifications do not (*ex hypothesi*) determine the line to which would be assigned the categories denoting the wives of the male positions of the line coinciding with the wife-givers of Ego's line. But there are specifications enough to determine which are the lines that would coincide with Ego's wife-givers and Ego's wife-takers.

In the Iatmül relationship terminology we find the same determination of lines coinciding with Ego's wife-givers and Ego's wife-takers, and the same indetermination concerning the 'wife-giver' lines of Ego's 'wife-giver' lines, and the 'wife-taker' lines of Ego's 'wife-taker' lines.

The indications of prescription can be seen in the following equations derived from the Iatmül terminology:

   (i) W = FFW = FMBSD = WBSD (*tagwa; iai*)[11]
  (ii) M = SW = MBSD (*nyame*)
 (iii) ZH = ZSS (*lando*)
  (iv) FZH = DH (*nondu*)
   (v) MB = MBSS = SWB (*wau*)
  (vi) FZC = DC (*na*)

These equations indicate that each term has both consanguineal and affinal specifications following the principle of asymmetry and in alternating genealogical levels.

There is no specification of the genealogical level to which Ego's *iairagwa* (*iai* wife) belongs because *iai* is actually specified as 'all women of the same patrilineal clan' as FM (1936: 308). But the *iai* of Ego's genealogical level can be identified by the terms employed in addressing her father (*naisagut*) or brother (*tawontu*). As the terms for the male positions alternate by genealogical level, the level of the woman can be defined by reference to these.

X

If actual alliances among the Iatmül were contracted in accordance with their relationship terminology,[12] it could be expected that marriages would occur with *iai* belonging to the same genealogical level or to the second descending genealogical level. This is a trait of other systems with alternation of terms by genealogical levels such as, for instance, the Dieri. This feature is compatible with the type of terminology because the second descending level reproduces Ego's level, as Ego's level reproduces the second ascending level. But such marriages are not reported in the Iatmül ethnography.

Marriage with the *iai* specified as FMBSD is, as Bateson himself seems to suggest,[13] totally consistent with the relationship terminology. If consistently observed, this kind of marriage would lead, contrary to what Bateson thinks in this respect (1936: 249), to a closed system of alliances, as the diagram of the relationship

---

[11] *iai* = 'all women of the same patrilineal clan' such as FM, FMBSD, etc.; sister of MBSS, *tawontu* (1936: 308).
[12] Bateson had 'no statistics' and made no 'random samples' of Iatmül behaviour (1936: 87 n. 1).
[13] 'The whole kinship vocabulary would point to the *iai* system as the older, and the concept of exchange of women may well have been adopted from neighbouring peoples' (1936: 90 n. 1).

terminology (*Figure 22*) shows. It would lead to an asymmetric system defined by five patrilineal descent lines. The closed system implicit in the Iatmül terminology can be represented as in *Figure 24*.[14] There are five lines: A, B, C, D, and E, related in such a way that A takes wives from B and C, B from C and D, C from D and E, E from A and B, in alternate genealogical levels.[15] The prescribed category is specified by reference to the second ascending level by means of the specification FMBSD, because it is this level that is reproduced at Ego's level.

Figure 24 Asymmetric prescriptive system with five lines and alternation by genealogical levels

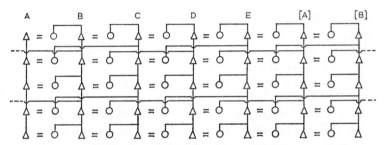

Note: lines A and B are duplicated in order to demonstrate more clearly the closure of the cycles

As in a four-line symmetric prescriptive terminology, Ego is related neither to the line to which the category specified as M belongs, nor to the line to which the category specified as F belongs. The alternation of terms by genealogical levels probably derives, as in the Dieri and in the Aranda terminologies, from this fact.

[14] For a good representation of the system in *Figure 10*, Layard's technique of circular diagrams should be adopted. Oddly enough, it was Bateson who suggested to Layard this technique 'by which a sheet of paper is rolled so as to form a cylinder round something hard, such as a jam jar, so as to provide a surface for writing' (Layard 1942: 113). As Bateson thought that his own case (Iatmül) was different from the Australian systems because it was not *closed* (1936: 248-9), he did not try to represent it with his 'cylindrical' technique that seems so appropriate for the Iatmül.

[15] The difference between this kind of system and an asymmetric system with five lines but without alternation, e.g. that of the Kachin (cf. Leach 1954), is that in the former system the five lines are formally necessary for the determination of Ego's 'wife-taker' and 'wife-giver' lines, whereas in the latter they are not.

H

The Iatmül relationship terminology can be represented in a diagram such as in *Figure 22*, which can be superposed on the ideal system shown in *Figure 24*. As we have seen, all the indications provided by the ethnography are consistent with such a representation. There are two types of unidirectional cycles of alliance relating the five lines in a consistently asymmetric way in alternate genealogical levels. One type of cycle links adjacent lines; the other links alternate lines. There is one prescribed category (*iai*) which is consistent with the disposition of all the terms in such a diagram.

XI

The Iatmül relationship terminology corresponds formally to some of the Iatmül actual institutions. The patrilineal clans coincide with the patrilines, and the *mbapma* with the alternation of terms in each patriline. Bateson states, as we have seen above, that the *mbapma* system does not control marriage (1932a: 269), but it is now clear that if marriages were contracted according to the prescribed category (*iai*), the *mbapma* system could be useful in categorizing people on the ground regarding these marriages. The people of one clan belonging to one *mbapma* should marry women from a different clan from the people belonging to the other *mbapma*. On the other hand, even though the terms used for feminine positions do not alternate, the women of alternate generations could be easily discriminated in relation to the *mbapma*, as well as by reference to *naisagut* and *tawontu*.

There is no indication in the terminology of any formal distinction coinciding with the totemic moieties. The difference in their relative importance for the different villages could indicate that they are not a decisive factor in Iatmül social classification regarding marriage. The relationship terminology, on the other hand, seems to be uniformly applied in the different villages.

The alternation of terms in the relationship terminology and the division of clans into *mbapma* are only two of the contexts in which Bateson sees the pattern of alternation applied. There are two other contexts: the alternation of initiatory grades and the alternation of siblings. There is also a further context in which he is 'tempted to see a development of the same type of pattern, namely . . . the structure of the flute music' (1936: 246).

The initiatory system is described by Bateson as constituted by two cross-cutting initiatory moieties (Ax, Ay, Bx, By). 'Each quadrant is divided into three named generation groups: 1, 3, 5, or 2, 4, 6; such that 1 are the fathers of 3, who are the fathers of 5; while 2 are the fathers of 4, who are the fathers of 6' (1936: 245). The principle of alternation is indeed applied in the relationship between generation groups, but the whole system of initiation, as described by Bateson, is difficult to grasp. The initiatory moieties are arranged in such a way that one moiety is always senior to the other (A senior to B, for instance), and that the members of Ax initiate the members of By, while the members of Ay initiate the members of Bx (1936: 245). But from his account, both in the 1932 article and in the 1936 book, it is impossible to gather what is the principle by which people of the A moiety, for instance, are divided into Ax and Ay, or who initiates the people belonging to Ax and Ay.

Regarding siblings, Bateson says that 'in large families in which there is a long series of brothers, the same sort of alternation is expected' (1936: 246). There are in Iatmül vocabulary five terms to designate the first, second, third, fourth, and fifth child. In their quarrels over the patrimony it is expected that the first and the third brothers will join forces against the second and the fourth (1936: 246).

Bateson's idea of explaining the structure of the flute music by the application of the principle of alternation is based on the fact that 'among the Iatmül the flute is always a duet instrument' (1935: 158). The flutes are always played in pairs and in each pair one flute is one tone higher than the other. 'The flute of lower pitch is spoken of as the elder brother of the other, though for totemic purposes the pair of flutes is taken as a unit' (1936: 246).

Bateson does not mention the system of personal names when describing the application of the principle of alternation. But it seems that the principle is followed in this sphere too, since 'most of an individual's names are passed to him from his father's father' (1932b: 403). The names are received from the father, who applies the names of his father to his sons, and the names of his father's sister to his daughter. But there is another series of names which are received from the mother's clan. 'Every clan has a certain number of names which it gives to its *laua nyanggu* (sister's children)' (1932b: 410). These names are also in pairs, 'elder brother' and 'younger brother', and are so distributed to the children.

The system of personal names shows the same traits as the relationship terms and gives another clue to an understanding of the alternation by genealogical levels. A patrilineal and matrilineal principle are involved in both cases. The system of names seems to reinforce the fact that an individual is linked with both his father's and his mother's clans and thus should marry in a third one. The alternation of personal names in one's own clan seems to indicate which is this third clan.

XII

The system of prestations, on the other hand, supports the idea that the Iatmül system is not only ideally asymmetric, but that it was so in practice also.

Needham writes that in prescriptive alliance systems there are some traits which although 'not diagnostic of this type of social organization, . . . taken in connection with the defining character of the terminology of social classification . . . make up a complex of institutions that is significantly coherent'. In an asymmetric system these traits are: (1) arranged marriages, (2) corporate involvement of descent groups in marriage payments, (3) widow inheritance, (4) sororal polygyny, (5) absence of divorce (cf. Needham 1963: 232), and (6) 'masculine' and 'feminine' goods which are exchanged between descent groups at the contraction of marriage (Needham 1970a: 257).

Among the Iatmül, not only are marriages arranged (cf. 1932a: 280) but the system of alliances also involves, as a consequence of the existence of two ideal cycles which relate five groups, groups other than the wife's and husband's clans. The most prominent context in which one finds this system of prestations, expressed in the exchange of two kinds of goods, is marriage, which necessitates prestations between a man and his wife's clan (exchange between *lando*, ZH, and *tawontu*, WB).

Wife-givers present *food* (coconut, fowl, pig) as well as women; wife-takers present *valuables* (shell ornaments, labour, support in war, etc.). This division of symbolic goods resembles the common Southeast Asia classification into 'masculine' and 'feminine' prestations, the former being given to superiors and the latter to inferiors (cf. Needham 1960a: 93-5). The resemblance is strengthened by the fact that among the Iatmül the wife-givers, who receive the 'masculine' valuables, etc., are superior to their wifetakers who make the prestation. At the conclusion of a *naven* the shells are tied to a spear and are thus presented to the *wau* (1936: 14). In general, 'most' shells and ornaments are 'attached to weapons' (1932a: 279) when they are handed over – a fact which tends again to confirm (by comparative reference) their 'masculine' significance.

There are several instances in Bateson's account in which this kind of exchange is described. During the 'arrangement' of his marriage, a man 'made a big ceremonial present of shells and other valuables to the girl's parents'. The girl was 'very heavily ornamented from head to foot with valuables, while her companions carried large numbers of decorated useful objects – pots, fish traps, etc. – these being a reciprocal present to that which the husband had made to the girl's parents' (1932a: 281). The exchange of goods in the arrangement of a marriage is called *waingga*, which seems to mean literally 'purchase'.

'The wife's relatives have always the right to call on the husband for help in any task, like house building, for which a crowd of manual labourers is necessary. When the task is completed the wife's people will stand a small feast for the labourers or they will at least distribute coconuts to them' (1936: 79).

Another context in which this kind of exchange occurs is in the relationship between the *laua* (ZC) group and the *wau* (MB) group. 'A man will take steps to mark out his relationship to the *laua* group whose allegiance he specially desires' (1936: 95). The *wau* will give not only a name to the *laua* but also a gift of a coconut (1936: 95), i.e. he will give his ZS a present of the kind that wife-givers give to wife-takers. The *wau-nyame nampa*, MB and M people, give pigs to the *lanoa nampa*, H people, or *laua nyanggu*, ZC people (1936: 19). The *laua* presents valuables to his *wau* (1936: 13). If a man imparts his clan secrets and spells to his sister's son, 'the esoterica *must be ceremonially paid for* with shell valuables' (1936: 37; cf. 60). There are also presentations of valuables to the shamanic spirits, which are accompanied by the killing of a pig (1932b: 420). Bateson believes that this pig is eaten, as is usual among the Iatmül, by the *laua* of the clan to which the valuables are offered (cf. 1932b: 420 n. 57).

After the celebration of *naven*, a general presentation of food and valuables follows. On one of these occasions, 'eight pigs were killed and presented. Of these one was given by her *wau* to the little girl who had caught the fish. . . . Of the remaining pigs, three were given by *wau*s to classificatory *laua*s', another one to the donor's sister's husband (also a *laua*, cf. *Table* 7), another was given by a woman to her husband's sister's child (i.e. *mbora* to *nasa*). In the case of the little girl, her father presented valuables to her *wau* (1936: 19).

In all these *naven* presentations, the food is presented by the wife-giver clan (MB, WBW) to the wife-taker clan (ZS, ZD, HZC). This pattern of exchange between *wau* and *laua* is significantly reversed in a myth. In this narrative, *naven* is celebrated by a man's wife's brother and wife's father on the occasions of the birth of both his first and second children. These relatives present *valuables* to the husband, and he in return presents *food* to them. In reality, *naven* is not celebrated for the birth of the first child of a man, so that in the myth there is a complete reversal of the occasion for *naven* and of the kinds of goods normally presented by wife-givers to wife-takers and vice versa (1936: 48-9).

There are also presentations of valuables when offences are committed. In the case of homicide, the killer presents valuables to the victim's relatives (1936: 99), and 'homicidal ornaments are usually presented by his *lanoa nampa* (husband people) to the killer' as a symbol of 'the triumph of the maternal clan' (1936: 217). But in the case of a trespass, there is also a presentation of food. The offender has to kill a fowl and present coconuts to the owners. The coconuts and the fowl will be eaten by the *laua* of the clan which owns the land. The offender has to present a basket of valuables and a *tambointsha* to the spirits of the ancestors (*angk-au*) of the offended clan. *Tambointsha* are tassels of feathers tied to string: 'they are symbols of successful kills' (1936: 46 n. 1). The *angk-au* will take the 'soul' of the valuables and of the *tambointsha*, and after a few days the valuables will be returned to the trespasser (1936: 46).

Food seems to be the means by which a man is symbolically attached to his wife's clan and to his mother's clan. The counter-offering of valuables is apparently the way of counteracting the possible bad effects of such an attachment. If a man is affected by *nggambli* ('dangerous and infectious guilt'), this 'infection' will be passed on to his *lando*, ZH, only if the latter gives food to the former, but not if he presents valuables to him (1936: 54-8). So that there is an emphasis upon the one direction of the offerings of food (cf. 1936: 58 n. 1).

But there are some instances in which both food and valuables are presented at the same time to the same group. Apart from the case of the trespass and the presentation to the shamanic spirits already seen, Bateson refers to another situation in which this double offering of food and valuables occurs. Certain members of a clan had been killed. As a result of this, 'the names of those who were dead were "loose"', and the remaining members of the clan were endangered. There was then a ceremony in which a pig was ritually killed and offered to the members of the clan, 'each of whom set his foot on it in turn', and they were offered *Turbo* shells and ornaments as well (1932b: 426).[16]

There is another instance in Bateson's account in which valuables were passed in the opposite direction, i.e. from wife-givers to wife-takers. He refers to a case in which a man, after his father's death, bought his name and his father's sister's name, offering a *Turbo* shell to the latter. Bateson says that 'this piece of ceremonial is the only context' that he knows in which 'valuables are ceremonially given to members of own clan' (1936: 50 n. 1). In fact, the valuables seem to have been passed in an unusual direction,[17] but the woman who received them (FZ) was probably not a member of 'own clan' but of one of the wife-taker clans.

In general, however, the 'masculine' goods are presented by the wife-takers and the 'feminine' goods by the wife-givers. For instance, Bateson bought a pair of flutes which were presented to their owners by their 'sister's children' and were ornamented 'with shell work' (1935: 161). The prestations correlate with the fact that wife-givers are 'superior' to wife-takers and that the whole system tends to the arrangement of alliances between groups. 'A man should support his wife's people in all their quarrels, even against his own clan', says Bateson (1936: 80), and he adds that 'if all affinal linkages were observed no one would be able to quarrel with anyone else inside the community, and everybody would have to go everywhere and do everything with everybody else, since the genealogical links are actually ubiquitous' (1936: 93).

---

[16] Bateson does not say whether the pig was eaten or by whom it might be eaten.
[17] Perhaps this is an instance of the symbolic reversal which often marks practices concerning death. See Needham 1967b: 430-1.

The absence of divorce, a trait that is present in other asymmetric systems of prescriptive alliance, such as the Kachin (Leach 1961: 15), is also found among the Iatmül. The *iai* wife has not only 'special rights', but cannot be divorced either (1932b: 280).

XIII

If we revert to the question of 'preferences' among the Iatmül, we can understand why it was so difficult for Bateson to grasp what sort of a system the Iatmül had.

Rule (1), covering marriage with *iai* (FMBSD), is perfectly consistent with the ideal system derived from the Iatmül relationship terminology. As we have already seen, if marriages of this kind were regularly contracted, there would be no inconsistency between the actual system and the 'ideal system' implicit in the terminology. The five related clans would coincide with the five lines in the terminology; *lanoa nampa* (ZH clan) would be the same group as *laua nyanggu* ('Ego's classificatory *laua*'s' clan), and *iai nampa* (FM clan) the same as *towa-naisagut* (wife's clan). The system would then be a closed one, as shown in *Figure 24*.

If we consider rule (2), i.e. marriage with *na* (FZD), instead, the connection between the alliances it implies and the relationship terminology is quite different. If a marriage of this sort is contracted, one of the consequences is that the *towa-naisagut* clan (wife's clan) coincides with *kaishe nampa* clan (daughter's husband's clan). If subsequent marriages follow this one in the 'curious way' in which Bateson says this form of marriage is connected with the *iai* marriage (cf. *Figure 17*), in the second descending genealogical level with respect to this first marriage, not only would these two clans coincide but also *iai nampa* (FMBSD clan) would be confused with them. On the other hand, in this second descending genealogical level, Ego's mother's clan (*wau-mbuambo*) would be also superposed on his sister's husband's clan, e.g. *lanoa nampa*. This superposition, and the superposition of relationship terms it implies, would be totally inconsistent with the number and the specification of the terms. On the other hand, a series of marriages following this rule leads to a patrilateral system with a constant reversal in the direction of the cycles of alliances that is not very likely to be maintained (cf. *Figure 16*; cf. Needham 1958, 1961).

If the third rule (exchange of sisters) is followed, the super-position of related clans that it implies is *towa-naisagut* (wife's clan) and *lanoa nampa* (ZH clan), as can be derived from *Figure 20*. If this type of marriage were consistently followed in subsequent genealogical levels and in accordance with *iai* marriage, the resulting system would imply a superposition of the following clans: *towa-naisagut* (W clan), *lanoa nampa* (ZH clan), *iai nampa* (FFW clan), *kaishe nampa* (FZH clan), and *wau-mbuambo* (MB clan). In a system of this type, the Iatmül designations for related

Figure 25 Consequence of repeated FMBD marriage

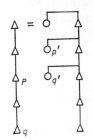

Note: *p* marries *p'*; *q* marries *q'*

clans seem redundant, and so for that matter does the Iatmül relationship terminology.

If the fourth rule ('*laua*'s son will marry *wau*'s daughter') were followed, it could not be regularly repeated, and would never lead to the constitution of a system.

The rule relates two lines and two consecutive genealogical levels, but if it were repeated the gap between the levels would increase by one for each second descending level (cf. *Figure 25*). Thus Ego's son's son in marrying his FMBD, would marry a woman belonging to Ego's level, and so on.

The repetition of this type of marriage would also have the consequence that a single wife-giving line would supply women to Ego's line in consecutive genealogical levels, which is inconsistent with the alternation otherwise characteristic of the Iatmül system. The same applies to the system derived from rule (3).

XIV

The Iatmül relationship terminology can be considered prescriptive and constituted by five lines with alternation of terms by genealogical levels (cf. *Figure 22*).

The first rule expressed by the Iatmül (marriage with *iai*, FMBSD) corresponds to this ideal system.

The second rule expressed (marriage with *na*, FZD) indicates a patrilateral asymmetric system constituted by three lines.

The third rule (exchange of sisters) implies a symmetric system with two lines.

The fourth rule ('*laua*'s son marries *wau*'s daughter') does not correspond to any system at all.

There are no records of actual marriages in the ethnography provided by Bateson. What he says, in fact, is that the Iatmül express certain rules of marriage and marry according to these rules or in any other way.

XV

In Lévi-Strauss's work there is no operational definition of 'preference'.

Regarding actual marriages he claims that, although 'the question of how far and in what proportion the members of a given society respect the norm is very interesting', this fact has nothing to do with the placing of this society in a typology (1967: xxi). So that, for the analysis of the 'elementary structure' under which the Iatmül system could be classified, the lack of records of actual marriages does not matter.

The four rules of the Iatmül, on the other hand, can each be properly considered as the 'desirable relationship' that Lévi-Strauss talks about (1967: xxii), and should thus provide for the classification of the 'structure'. The 'desirable relationship', he says, 'is a function of the social structure' and 'the spouse is the spouse solely because she belongs to an alliance category or stands in a certain kinship relationship to Ego' (1967: xxi-xxii). But which of the 'alliance categories' or 'kinship relationships' as expressed by the Iatmül (namely, *iai*, FMBSD; *na*, FZD; ZHZ; and *wau*'s daughter, FMBD) is a function of their social structure?

If, as Lévi-Strauss avers, there is no difference between 'prescription' and 'preference', then the four 'desirable relationships' should determine the classification of the structure.

'A preferential system is prescriptive when envisaged at the model level', says Lévi-Strauss (1967: xxi). Consequently the Iatmül must, from this point of view, have three different systems at this level: (1) an asymmetric model with five lines and alternation of terms by genealogical levels; (2) a patrilateral asymmetric model; and (3) a symmetric model. There is in addition a preference (4) that does not fit any systematic model.

If these different models, which may be derived from the various 'desirable relationships', are indeed a function of the Iatmül social structure, one is led to think either that the Iatmül possess four different social structures or that they possess an exceedingly complicated one which has apparently no analogues in the literature.

XVI

So far, we have been applying the 'solutions' proposed by Lévi-Strauss in the preface to the second French edition of *Les Structures élémentaires de la parenté* (1967). If instead we consider the preface to the first edition (1949), the 'solution' seems to be quite different.

According to his statements in this place, Lévi-Strauss would probably consider the Iatmül case as one of those 'hybrid and ambiguous forms . . . where there are several preferential solutions' (1949: x). In this case, it might not be considered an 'elementary structure'. But in this same preface an 'elementary structure' is defined as one class of systems which, 'while defining all members of the society as relatives, divide them into two categories, viz. possible spouses and prohibited spouses' (1949: ix). Since among the Iatmül 'by his genealogy at birth a man is provided with a series of relatives . . . with a complete set of relatives-in-law and potential wives' (Bateson 1932a: 263), it is difficult to see why, if this aspect of Iatmül society fits so perfectly with the very definition of an 'elementary structure', it should not in the end be considered as such.

XVII

The difficulties in classifying the Iatmül system according to Lévi-Strauss's definitions do not arise from an inherent ambiguity in Iatmül society, but from the inconsistency between definitions and classificatory criteria in Lévi-Strauss's writings.[18]

---

[18] Further on Lévi-Strauss's method and definitions, see Korn 1969a; Korn and Needham 1970.

Whereas he gives a formal, viz. terminological, criterion for the definition of an 'elementary structure', he gives far more weight to explicit rules or preferences when he actually classifies a system. The formal terminological criterion, moreover, seems to be completely forgotten by Lévi-Strauss when in 1967 he reconsiders the definition of an 'elementary structure'.

Following Kroeber and Hocart, Dumont and Needham, one can consider that the relationship terminology is a form of social classification implying an ideal mode of social organization. In the case of the Iatmül the form of classification and the principles involved are clear enough.[19] Why these principles are not systematically followed in the actual behaviour is another matter. The fact that the Iatmül express certain marriage preferences which conflict with their form of classification does not disable the analyst in classifying the ideal system.

Of course, it would be better to be able to know why this ideal system is not applied in practice. But the ethnography does not provide enough data for such an explanation. The number and the size of the villages that Bateson includes under the label of 'Iatmül society' could be one of the causes of the inconsistency. The asynchronous decay of Iatmül institutions (totemic moieties, ceremonial houses, division of clans, etc.) and the exchange of women between different villages has probably made it difficult to maintain the system. But the traces of prescriptive values among the Iatmül can still be found in Bateson's description. The special rights of the *iai* wife, as described above, seem to be one of them, and also the fact that the betrothal to *iai* takes place at a very early age (Bateson 1932a: 263 n. 8). The system of prestations, and the absence of divorce as far as the *iai* wife is concerned, are some more indications. Finally, the fact that they explain their use of the relationship terms by reference to *ngaiva*, patrilineal clan (1932a: 268), and that they do talk of 'wrong' marriages (1932a: 280) and 'wrong totemic group' (1932a: 285), indicates a prior

---

[19] Another aspect of Iatmül social classification that deserves mention is the *ethos*, the 'emotional content' of institutions, on which Bateson lays considerable stress. In particular, the culturally determined sentiments appropriate to the relationships MB/ZS, B/Z, F/S, and H/W appear respectively to be + + − −. (A plus sign denotes a relatively free and familiar relationship, a minus sign a relationship marked rather by reserve or antagonism.) In the light of a comparative survey of the social organization of the emotions this pattern can, it is claimed, be recognized as 'a standard patrilineal scheme' (Needham 1971a: liv-lv).

state in which the actual institutions may have corresponded more closely with the terminology.

XVIII

In the preface to the 1949 edition of *Les Structures élémentaires de la parenté*, Lévi-Strauss states that 'for the elucidation of any special problem that the reader has in mind, the definitions and distinctions used here should be applied, and the same method followed' (p. xi).

In the Dieri case, following his own method, Lévi-Strauss arrived at the conclusion that the Dieri were a case of 'transition' from 'generalized exchange' to 'restricted exchange', that their system was quite 'anomalous', that they exhibited the 'structure' of a moiety system and the rule of marriage of an 'Aranda system', and that their relationship terminology was properly represented in a diagram composed of four patrilines (1949: 256-62). In an independent analysis of the system (cf. chapter 4), however, we have found that they possessed a four-matriline symmetric prescriptive terminology, a set of matrilineal clans, matrilineal moieties, and a rule of marriage totally consistent with these features.

According to Lévi-Strauss, the Aranda possess matrilineal moieties and 'bilateral descent'. In chapter 2 we have shown that the ethnography reports patrilineal moieties, patrilineal member-ship in sections and subsections, and no matrilineal institutions or transmission of any sort.

A similar discrepancy between the 'findings' of Lévi-Strauss and of other analysts working on the same societies can be found in, for instance, Needham's analysis of the Wikmunkan (cf. Needham 1962b; Lévi-Strauss 1949; 262-70), in Needham's analysis of the Aimol (cf. Needham 1960c; Lévi-Strauss 1949: 330-2), and in Leach's observations on the Chin/Kachin case (Lévi-Strauss 1949: 289-327; Leach 1969b).[20]

In the case of the Iatmül system, we could not precisely follow Lévi-Strauss's particular method, because he did not analyse this

---

[20] In the second edition of *Les Structures élémentaires de la parenté* (1967) Lévi-Strauss ignores Needham's analysis, which is quite discrepant from his own, of the Wikmunkan system; yet he tacitly responds to Needham's critical observations on his analysis of the Aimol system by leaving this out altogether.

society; but we have seen what the conclusions would have to be if one tried to apply the 'definitions' and 'distinctions' that he alludes to. Our analysis has demonstrated that the Iatmül possess an asymmetric prescriptive terminology with five lines and alternation of terms by genealogical levels. Following Lévi-Strauss's definitions we should probably have arrived at the conclusion either that they represent a 'hybrid' case or that they had four different social structures.

But if our intention were to correct or discuss some points in Lévi-Strauss's work on elementary structures, it would in his view be an impossible task, since, as he says: 'even if some aspect of the problem treated in [this work] were developed no new idea would need to be introduced' (Lévi-Strauss 1949: xi).

Chapter Six

Some Comments on Alternation: the Mara Case

I

The Aranda, the Dieri, and the Iatmül terminologies have in common the following features: all of them are lineal; in all of them there is an alternation of terms in each line; and in all of them the prescribed category is genealogically specified as second cross-cousin (MMBDD, FFZSD, FMBSD, MFZDD).

We have so far considered Durkheim's hypothesis on the relationship between alternation and the concurrence of patrilocality and matrilineal descent, and Lévi-Strauss's reformulation of this hypothesis in terms of disharmonic regimes and symmetry.

From the three cases studied the only one that is consistent with such hypotheses is the Dieri, because this system is patrilocal and has matrilineal moieties and matrilineal exogamous clans. The Aranda and the Iatmül, however, cannot be explained by the same hypothesis. In the Aranda case, there are patrilocal groups, patrilineal affiliation to the four sections or the eight subsections, and a terminology composed of four patrilines. In the Iatmül case, there are patrilineal clans, patrilineal non-exogamous totemic moieties, patrilineal ceremonial moieties, patrilocal groups, and five patrilines in the terminology.

Patrilocality and matrilineal descent cannot therefore be considered to stand in any necessary relationship to alternation.

Dumont and, following him, Sperber, have latterly proposed an alternative explanation for this sort of system. We shall analyse this in the last section of the present chapter.

Lévi-Strauss also proposed another possible evolutionary sequence in the formation of alternating systems, but in his case it was not because he rejected his former proposal on the relation between regimes and structures. His second hypothesis about the factors producing alternation is, as we shall now see, complementary rather than alternative to the first.

II

For Lévi-Strauss, 'the system of alternate generations does not result exclusively, or necessarily, from bilateral descent. It is also an immediate function of patrilateral marriage' (1949: 254). Also: 'patrilateral marriage *systems* and disharmonic regimes are both of the alternating *type*' and 'this alternating type, which is common to both, makes the transition from the patrilateral systems to the formula for restricted exchange easier than it is for matrilateral systems' (1949: 275).

None of the three systems we have already considered seems to have evolved from a patrilateral system (marriage with the category specified as FZD). None of them can be characterized, either, as possessing 'bilateral' – i.e. bilineal – descent. Only the Dieri can be classified as having a 'disharmonic regime'. The Aranda and the Iatmül certainly function according to a 'harmonic' regime.

But for Lévi-Strauss the case that illustrates the passage from a patrilateral system to a 'formula of restricted exchange' is the Mara system.

The Mara are, he says, one of the group of tribes that have 'a kinship terminology of the Aranda type, but with only four named divisions. . . . The son remains in his father's division, and this gives the four divisions the appearance of patrilineal lines grouped by pairs into two moieties' (1949: 248). Radcliffe-Brown and Warner, says Lévi-Strauss, 'have tried to bring the social structure and the kinship terminology into harmony' (1949: 248-9) because they considered that the four divisions of the Mara are four 'semi-moieties' consisting each of two groups which are equivalent to subsections among the Aranda. But for Lévi-Strauss, 'the question must be asked whether the Mara system . . . should not be interpreted . . . as a system effectively with four classes and a borrowed Aranda-type terminology'. In support of this argument he says that 'if the Mara system differed from an Aranda system only in that subsections were unnamed, the rules of marriage would be strictly identical in both. But this is not so' (1949: 249).

Lévi-Strauss bases this statement on the fact that, in addition to their rule of a normal Aranda type, there is an alternative marriage formula in the Mara-type systems studied by Sharp in Northwestern Queensland. Lévi-Strauss notes that the Laierdila system of the islands and coast of Queensland, studied by Sharp, are 'of the Mara type' but that it has two additional marriage possibilities, one with the mother's brother's son's daughter, and the other with the father's father's sister's daughter. For the Laierdila, then, 'it is . . . possible for an A_1 man to marry a woman of any of the subsections B_1, B_2, C_1, C_2 or any woman of the moiety opposite to his own' (Sharp 1935: 162). He notes then that 'the question arises seriously whether the Mara system . . . should not . . . be considered as a four-class system with patrilateral marriage, . . . expressed in terms of an Aranda-type system'. Also, 'the Mara system, because it has kept to its primitive structure, has had to allow its patrilateral orientation to be submerged in the apparently bilateral form of its alternate marriage, which is of the Kariera type' (1949: 251). Therefore, 'until more information is available, the Mara system should not be regarded as an Aranda system which has lost some of its superficial characteristics, but as an original and heterogeneous system upon which Aranda features are gradually being superimposed' (1949: 252).

III

The Mara were included by Spencer in the category of 'tribes with direct male descent'. He describes them as having a system composed of two patrilineal moieties, Muluri and Umbana, each of which is subdivided into two 'classes'. These named 'classes' are Murungun and Mumbali, in the Muluri moiety, and Purdal and Kuial, in the Umbana moiety. 'Though there are no distinct names for them, each class is really divided into two groups – the equivalent of the subclasses in the Aranta and Warramunga. They are, in fact, precisely similar to the unnamed groups into which each class is divided in the southern half of the Arunta and in the Warrai tribe' (Spencer 1914: 60-1). According to Spencer, each of the subdivisions of the four named divisions can be distinguished by the letters α and β, so that the intermarrying groups and the classes of the children can be represented as follows (see *Table 8*). The explanation is that a Murungun α man must marry a Purdal α woman and their children are Murungun β. A Purdal α man marries a Murungun α woman and their children are Purdal β, etc.

I

Table 8 Spencer's representation of the intermarrying groups among the Mara (Spencer 1914: 61, Table 3)

Moiety 1 Muluri	Moiety 2 Umbana	Children	Children
Murungun α	Purdal α	Murungun β	Purdal β
Murungun β	Kuial β	Murungun α	Kuial α
Mumbali α	Kuial α	Mumbali β	Kuial β
Mumbali β	Purdal β	Mumbali α	Purdal α

In 1904, Spencer and Gillen gave a detailed account of the Mara relationship terminology (cf. *Table 9*). According to these authors, the relationship terms are perfectly consistent with the arrangement of the named classes and unnamed subclasses. The diagram in which these terms can be arranged is composed of four lines (see *Figure 26*).

Figure 26 Mara relationship terminology (Spencer and Gillen 1904: cf. *Table 9*)

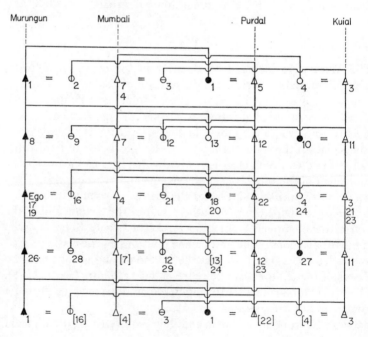

Table 9

Mara Relationship Terms
(Spencer and Gillen 1904)*

1.	*muri-muri*	FF, FFB, FFZ, WFM, SS, SD
2.	*namini*	FM, FMZ
3.	*napitjatja*	MF, FFZSWF, DHF, DC
4.	*unkuku* or *kuku*	MM, FFZSWF, FFZDC, SWM
5.	*nakaka*	MMB (w.s.)
6.	*umburnati*	WFF
7.	*tjumalunga*	WMF, WMB
8.	*naluru*	F, FB
9.	*katjirri*	M, MZ
10.	*umburnana*	FZ
11.	*gnagun*	MB, DH
12.	*nipari*	WF, ZHF, FFZS, FFZD, FMBS, FMBD, ZS, ZD
13.	*gnungatjulunga*	WM, ZHM, FFZSW, FMBSW
14.	*yallnalli*	HF
15.	*niringwinia-arunga*	HM
16.	*irrimakula*	W, WZ, H, HB
17.	*guauaii*	eB, FeBS
18.	*gnarali*	eZ
19.	*niritja*	yB, FyBS
20.	*gnanirritja*	yZ, FyBD
21.	*nirri-marara*	MBC, FZC
22.	*mimerti*	WB
23.	*kati-kati*	SWF
24.	*gnakaka*	DHM
25.	*nirri-miunka-karunga*	HZ
26.	*nitjari*	S, BS
27.	*gnaiiati*	D, BD
28.	*nirri-lumpa-karunga*	SW
29.	*gnaiawati*	ZD
30.	*tjamerlunga*	DH (w.s.)
31.	*naningurara*	SW (w.s.)
32.	*yillinga*	SC (w.s.)
33.	*gambiriti*	SSC
34.	*kankuti*	DDC
35.	*yallnali*	SSS (w.s.)

* Spencer and Gillen 1904: 87, 88, Table of Descent: Mara Tribe (op. p. 87), 130, 131.

Although Spencer and Gillen's account of the Mara relationship terms is very detailed, it still seems to be incomplete with regard to the specifications of some categories. Yet the arrangement of the terms does not differ from that of the Aranda terms, and the prescribed category (*irrimakula*) is genealogically specified as MMBDD/FFZSD, i.e. the same as the prescribed category among the Aranda and the Dieri.

A man is betrothed to one or several women who are *irrimakula* to him. This betrothal is arranged by the father of the woman '[telling] a man who stands in the relationship of father's sister's son to the individual to whom the former proposes to give his daughter. This telling another man who acts as intermediary is associated with the strongly marked avoidance of son-in-law and father-in-law in the Mara tribe' (Spencer and Gillen 1904: 77 n. 1). Thus the individuals who arrange the betrothal of a man are *nipari* (FMBS, WF) and *nirri-marara* (FZS) to him.

Although it is the 'general rule' to marry a *irrimakula*, there is a further 'lawful' wife for a man. A man may marry, namely, a woman who stands in the position of *nirri-marara*, FZD/MBD, to him, provided she comes from a distant locality (Spencer and Gillen 1904: 126).

IV

Warner's report on the Mara 'semi-moieties' (1933) does not differ from Spencer and Gillen's account of the Mara 'marriage classes'. When describing the tribes of the Gulf of Carpentaria and the mouth of the Roper River, he says:

> each tribe has four named divisions, but instead of the son being in a different division from his father, as in the normal section systems, he remains in the same group. If the father is P, the son is P. This gives each of the four patrilineal lines a name and creates a condition where there are two named divisions in each tribe.

> Marriage is exogamous. Ego cannot marry into his own or the group belonging to his side of the tribe. Not only is he excluded from these two groups, but he cannot marry into his mother's group of the opposite moiety (Warner 1933: 79).

The list of terms he reports for the Mara is as in *Table 10*.

This list is not totally consistent with the list in Spencer and
Gillen. There are fewer terms; certain distinctions by sex at the
same genealogical level are lacking; there is only one term for

Table 10

Mara Relationship Terms

(Warner 1933: op. p. 69)

1.	*mur-ĭ-mur-ĭ*	FF, FFZ, SS, SD
2.	*mi-mi*	FM, FMB, FMBSSSS, FMBSSSD
3.	*bĭ-dja-dja*	MF, MFZ, DS, DD
4.	*go-go*	MM, MMB, MMBSS, MMBSD, MMBSSSS, MMBSSSD
5.	*lur-lu*	F, FB
6.	*kai-djĭr-ri*	M, MZ
7.	*bar-nan-a*	FZ
8.	*gar-dī-gar-dī*	MB, MBSS, MBSD
9.	*mu-lor-ī*	MMBS, MMBD, MMBSSS, MMBSSD
10.	*nī-pal-lī*	FMBS, FMBD, FMBSSS, FMBSSD
11.	*baba*	eB
12.	*nua-ru-nur-no*	eZ
13.	*lĭm-bil'-li*	yB, yZ
14.	*um-bar'-na*	FMBSS
15.	*na-mai-gor'-la*	W, FMBSD
16.	*ma-gar-ra*	MBS, MBD
17.	*nī-djal'-lī*	S, D

yB and yZ against two in Spencer and Gillen, one term for FM
and WFF against two in Spencer and Gillen, etc. The spelling
also is very different. But, still, this list can be arranged in the
same kind of diagram and is even more consistent with it and more
economical (*see Figure 27*).

V

We are now in a position to review Lévi-Strauss's assertions about
the Mara system and, consequently, to judge the validity of his
hypothesis about patrilateral systems as a basis for alternation.

  1 In the Mara system there are four lines; these are named and
grouped into two moieties. The fact that 'the son remains in his

father's division' does not 'give the four divisions the appearance of patrilineal lines grouped by pairs into two moieties' (Lévi-Strauss 1949: 248). The four divisions coincide with the four lines, and it is indifferent in this case whether these divisions are considered as an additional feature or as the same entity, under another aspect, as the four lines. The fact is that what we call lines are special groupings of Mara categories which the Mara themselves actually distinguish by name. In this sense,

Figure 27 Mara relationship terminology (Warner 1933, cf. *Table 10*)

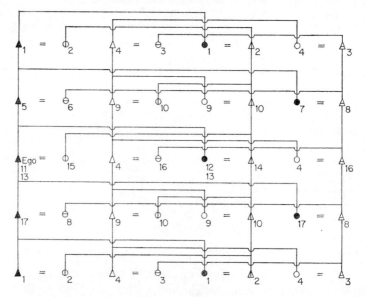

the named lines of the Mara are no different from those of the Iatmül.

2 The Mara system does not differ from the Aranda system in its rules of marriage. In both systems the prescribed category is, contrary to Lévi-Strauss's assertion, 'strictly identical'. In both cases this category is genealogically specified as MMBDD, FFZSD, FMBSD, MFZDD.

The alternative marriageable category is that specified as MBD, FZD, as is consistent with a system composed basically of exogamous moieties. In this respect, the Mara do not differ from the Dieri, i.e. when a person of the right category is not available for betrothal, the second choice is a person of the other category of the same genealogical level in the opposite moiety.

3 There is no evidence whatever of a previous 'patrilateral orientation' which is now 'submerged in the apparently bilateral form' of the alternate marriage among the Mara (cf. Lévi-Strauss 1949: 251). Both the prescribed category and the alternative 'lawful' category are strictly bilateral because of the symmetry of the system.

The Laierdila case, studied by Sharp (1935), does not add any relevant clue in support of Lévi-Strauss's idea of a previous 'patrilateral orientation'. Among the Laierdila also, the terminology consists of four lines; there are eight sections arranged into two exogamous groups; and the alternative marriages are, as among the Mara, with categories belonging to the opposite major division. The difference from the Mara system is that the Laierdila allow marriage with categories belonging to consecutive genealogical levels, i.e. MBSD and FFZD (also FMBD). Both of these categories belong to the opposite division, and neither of them reflects a 'patrilateral orientation' but only the fact that there are two major exogamous divisions.

4 The Mara system should not be considered as 'an Aranda system which has lost some of its superficial characteristics', as Lévi-Strauss quite correctly points out, though it must be said that nobody has ever suggested this possibility. But neither should it be regarded as 'an original and heterogeneous system upon which Aranda features are gradually being imposed' (1949: 252). Again, Lévi-Strauss maintains that the Mara system should be regarded 'as a system effectively with four classes and a borrowed Aranda-type terminology' (1949: 249). But there is no reason to conceive the system in this way either. As for the further suggestion by Lévi-Strauss, the conclusion should be again negative: one could not possibly consider the Mara system 'as a four-class system with patrilateral marriage, . . . expressed in terms of an Aranda type system' (1949: 251).

There are three main reasons for rejecting all of Lévi-Strauss's suggestions:

(i) the Mara system, as we have already seen, has a terminology the features of which are exactly the same as in the Aranda;

(ii) the distribution of categories in the Mara four divisions has nothing to do with the distribution of categories in a so-called four-class system. The Kariera (a 'four-class' system) have a two-line terminology, and positions in consecutive genealogical

Figure 28 Difference between the distribution of divisions by lines in the Kariera system (*Figure 28a*) and the lines of the Mara system (*Figure 28b*)

Figure 28a

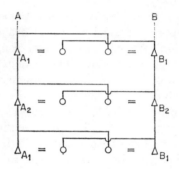

Figure 28b

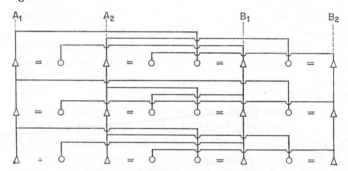

Note: A_1, A_2, B_1, B_2 correspond to the named divisions

levels of each line belong to different sections, so that the four sections are grouped into two main divisions coinciding with the two lines. The Mara have instead a four-line terminology; consecutive positions in each line are grouped in the same named division; and the difference between the correspondence of lines, divisions, and grouping of consecutive positions in each line can be seen in *Figure 28*;

(iii) as we have already seen in (3) above, there is nothing in the Mara system that can be assimilated to 'patrilateral marriage', nor is there any indication that this was a prior stage in the evolution of Mara marriage regulations.

VI

The Mara relationship terminology, as a mode of social classification, does not differ from that of the Aranda. Moreover, the four cases examined here, namely, Aranda, Dieri, Iatmül, and Mara, can be classified together by some of the basic principles that they apply, i.e. (1) all of them are lineal, (2) all of them present the features of a closed classification, (3) in all of them the prescribed category can be defined by the relations of alliance of one line with respect to two other lines.

Figure 29 The prescribed category in alternating systems

Figure 29a Matrilines   *Figure 29b* Patrilines

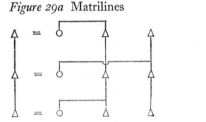 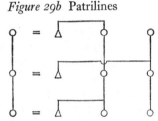

For each line, the principle involved in the determination of the prescribed category can be represented as follows (see *Figure 29*). Consecutive positions in one line are related affinally to two different lines. The number of lines – four as in the Aranda, the Dieri, and the Mara, and five as in the Iatmül – derives from the principle of symmetry or asymmetry in force.

The alternation of terms in each line can then be seen as a result of three factors: (i) a lineal classification, (ii) a closed classification, and (iii) a principle according to which a line cannot be affinally related to the same line in two consecutive genealogical positions.

This negative factor (iii) can be seen as a matrilineal principle applied to a terminology composed of patrilines, or as a patrilineal principle applied to a terminology composed of matrilines.

Whether such an approach can be regarded as a reversion to the theory of alternation as a consequence of 'double descent' depends very much on what is meant by 'descent'. Formally speaking, the descent lines in the terminologies considered are either patrilines (Aranda, Mara, Iatmül) or matrilines (Dieri), and very clearly so; in other words, the terminologies cannot be coherently organized on the basis of lines of the opposite kind. The social organization of these societies is consistent with these formal traits. Membership in exogamous groups such as sections, subsections, and moieties among the Aranda, the so-called semi-moieties among the Mara, the totemic clans and moieties among the Dieri, and the *ngaiva* and initiatory groups and moieties among the Iatmül, is determined by the same principle as is expressed in the terminological lines of each of them. Except for the fact that residence is patrilocal among the Dieri, there does not exist in any of the societies considered any 'bundle of rights' of comparable significance transmitted in the line opposite to that on which the terminology is based. 'Double descent' or 'implicit matrilineal moieties', in the case of the Aranda or the Mara, is a complicated way of saying that an individual is not affinally related to the line to which his mother belongs. The same holds for 'patrilineal moieties' among the Dieri. This agrees with Dumont's point, in discussing the validity of Radcliffe-Brown's explanation of 'alternation' by the superposition of patrilineal and matrilineal moieties (either 'real', 'implicit', 'latent', or 'underlying'), that 'it would seem that Australians nowhere recognize a *double* set of moieties'. But, in the light of the examples analysed here, it cannot be agreed that systems of alternating generations are to be explained by 'intermarriage between sections in preference to hypothetical holistic matrilineal descent' (Dumont 1966: 249).

The fact is that 'sections' are not a necessary institution for this kind of system. They do not exist among the Mara any more than they exist among the Dieri, yet these systems are no different from that of the Aranda. It is true that Dumont, when giving this explanation, is considering the Kariera, the Aranda, and the Murngin, all of which do possess sections. But as sections are not present in all alternating systems, they cannot be accepted as 'the real agent' (Dumont 1966: 249) of these systems. On the other hand, if the Kariera and the Aranda are similar because they possess sections, they differ in their forms of social classification.

In the Kariera system the alternation is given by the fact that people of consecutive genealogical levels belong to different sections. This fact does not produce in the Kariera system any modification with respect to the line to which each category is affinally related. In this terminology there are only two lines, and people of consecutive genealogical levels do marry in the same line. The sort of alternation involved in the Kariera system is thus different from that which characterizes the Aranda, Mara, Dieri, or Iatmül systems. It could even be said that the sort of alternation in a Kariera system is purely symbolic, i.e. the mode of classification involved with reference to alliances between lines does not differ from that of a two-line symmetric terminology in which consecutive genealogical levels are not distributed among sections. The prescribed category is the same, and there is no alternation of lines to which two consecutive positions are affinally related.

The four cases that we have examined can be defined by a principle such as that represented in *Figure 29*. Whether patrilineal or matrilineal, symmetric or asymmetric, with sections or without, this mode of articulation is present in all of them. In this respect, it is not possible, either, to agree with the two 'generalizations' expressed by Sperber, who, following Dumont, asserts that:

(1) There is no alternation of generations without a partition of the population into classes, according to which the men from one class marry in only one other class.
(2) There is no partition into classes without symmetry according to which the men and women from class A marry in the same class B (Sperber 1968: 185).

First of all, the cases of the Mara, the Dieri, and the Iatmül, which do not have any 'partition into classes', refutes generalization (1). The implication derived from (1) and (2), namely: 'there is no alternation without symmetry', is refuted by the case of the Iatmül.

Chapter Seven

Permutation Models and Prescriptive Systems

I

The Appendix to the first part of *Les Structures élémentaires de la parenté* written by André Weil on the 'Algebraic Study of Certain Types of Marriage (Murngin System)' (Lévi-Strauss 1949: 278-85), inaugurated a series of articles on the mathematical treatment of marriage rules.[1]

The goals of such an effort are not self-evident. According to Piaget, Lévi-Strauss 'has succeeded in discerning, in various kinship organizations, algebraical network structures and transformation groups, etc., which he has been able to formalize with the aid of mathematicians such as A. Weil and G. Th. Guilbaud' (1968: 92). Weil himself states that the purpose of his work is 'to show how a certain type of marriage laws can be interpreted algebraically, and how algebra and the theory of groups of substitutions can facilitate its study and classification' (Weil 1949: 278). In Kemeny, Snell, and Thompson (1957: 343-53) the emphasis is didactic, and concentrates on how permutation matrices serve also to represent marriage rules in primitive societies. For Bush, 'when the rules of marriage and descent are sufficiently specific and unique we might expect to describe the system mathematically' (Bush 1963: 159).

We intend to analyse here some of the works dealing with the mathematical expression of marriage rules (Weil 1949; Kemeny, Snell, and Thompson 1957; Bush 1963; White 1963; Courrège 1965) and to do so by considering them under several aspects: (1) the purposes of mathematical translation of this sort; (2) the premises on which the different works are based; (3) the relevance of the empirical examples adduced.

[1] This chapter constitutes my contribution to Korn and Needham 1970.

II

All the works mentioned above are concerned primarily with the mathematical expression of 'marriage rules'. A mathematical expression of a social phenomenon of any sort constitutes, in the first place, a translation into a formal notation. The possible purposes of translating in general would seem to be: (i) to communicate with a public who do not understand the original; (ii) to record or transmit information in a more synthetic form of expression; and (iii) to express a certain content in a language permitting operations to be carried out that are not possible by means of the language in which that content was originally expressed.

The general content and presentation of the works under consideration are very similar and consist of a number of conditions and axioms describing the sort of system and units they are going to deal with, the mathematical devices they employ to represent rules of marriage and descent, and some examples of their application to the data on concrete societies.

Let us summarize the specific content of each of the works, and then try to assess which of the possible purposes of a translation they fit.

III

Weil (1949) deals with societies in which:

> the individual men and women are divided into classes, each person's class being determined, according to certain rules, by those of his parents. According to the respective classes of a man and of a woman, the marriage rules indicate whether they can marry or not (Weil 1949: 278).

He also postulates two conditions:

> (*A*) For any individual, man or woman, there is one and only one type of marriage which he (or she) has the right to contract.
> (*B*) For any individual, the type of marriage which he (or she) may contract depends solely on sex and the type of marriage from which he (or she) is descended (Weil 1949: 279).

He proposes '$f(M_i)$' as the notation for the type of marriage of a son descended from marriage M_i, and the notation '$g(M_i)$' as that for the type of marriage of a daughter descended from the same type M_i. Knowledge of the two functions f and g, he says 'completely determines the marriage rules in the society studied' (Weil 1949: 279).

Weil then presents three examples: (1) a society with four classes and generalized exchange (p. 279); (2) a society with four classes and restricted exchange (280-1); and (3) a society with eight classes and two 'marriage formulas' to be applied alternatively (281-5). He demonstrates in each case how $f(M_i)$, i.e. son's marriage type, and $g(M_i)$, i.e. daughter's marriage type, can be expressed as permutations of the set parent's marriage types $(M_i...M_n)$. He also demonstrates that in the third case marriage with father's sister's daughter, expressed by the formula

$$f[f(M_i)] = g\,[g(M_i)],$$

is not possible.

IV

Bush (1963)[2] works with societies in which:

> rather specific clans, moieties, generations, etc., are culturally defined for each man, his wife and his children. This permits us to distinguish a specified number of possible *marriage types* and to deduce from the ethnographic material the allowed marriage type of a man or woman when we know the marriage type of his or her parents (Bush 1963: 159).

He introduces the notions of matrix (p. 161), permutation operator (p. 161), vector (p. 161), cyclic group (p. 162), commutation of two operators (p. 162), and some others, which he applies to the Kariera, the Tarau, and the Aranda systems. In the first case, viz. Kariera, applying different operations to the matrices representing parents' type of marriage and children's type of marriage, he reaches the 'interpretation' that:

[2] The date of composition of Bush's work is unknown. White, who describes it as a 'pioneer' piece on the mathematics of kinship (1963: viii), published it for the first time as an appendix to his own book (159-72). He supplies no information on its previous circulation. It was certainly written after 1949, since it refers to *Les Structures élémentaires de la parenté*, and evidently before 1957, when Kemeny, Snell, and Thompson acknowledge their obligation to 'the work of . . . Robert Bush' (1957: 343).

my daughter's son and my son's daughter may contract the same type of marriage and hence may marry one another (p. 166),

and, further, that

I belong to the same class as my daughter's son's daughter's son if I am a man or to my son's daughter's son's daughter if I am a woman (p. 166).

As for the Tarau, Bush gives the names of what he calls their 'four classes', and the rules of marriage and descent, and 'deduces' that

a child is always of the same class as his or her father (p. 167);
cross-cousin marriage is permissible (p. 167);
my daughter's daughter's daughter's daughter must contract the same type of marriage as I have (p. 168).

In the case of the Aranda, he describes them as having eight classes and again 'deduces' that

my daughter's son's son may marry my son's daughter, i.e. . . . a man may marry his father's mother's brother's son's daughter (p. 170);
my daughter's son's daughter may marry my son's son's son (p. 171);
a man can marry his mother's father's sister's daughter's daughter (p. 171).

V

Kemeny, Snell, and Thompson deal with 'Marriage Rules in Primitive Societies' in sections 7 and 8 of the seventh chapter of their book *Finite Mathematics* (1957). According to White, these brief sections 'are a major advance over the previous work (viz. Weil 1949)' (White 1963: 32), because the properties of the societies to be investigated are formulated as an integrated set of axioms.

In the first section devoted to marriage rules (section 7, pp. 343-8), their seven axioms postulate conditions that do not differ from those proposed by Weil. They indicate, as in Weil's work, that 'each member of the society is assigned a marriage type' (Kemeny, Snell, and Thompson 1957: 343 [Axiom 1]). They adopt the same mathematical device as Bush proposes, and they give a number of problems to be solved by the reader, again using as examples the Kariera and the Tarau systems. The problems posed are of this form: given the 'marriage types' of parents, sons, and daughters, find the 'rules' that allow cross-cousin marriage, for instance, or the matrices that represent rules of descent and 'marriage type' of sons and daughters.

In the second section devoted to the subject (section 8, pp. 348-53) they consider the axioms 5, 6, and 7 proposed in the previous section. They present for each of the axioms the expressions that represent them in terms of matrices representing son's marriage type and daughter's marriage type. Axiom 6, for example, which states that 'in particular, no man is allowed to marry his sister' (p. 343), requires, they say, that $S^{-1}D$ be a complete permutation, which is an immediate consequence of the fact that the matrix of the brother–sister relationship is $S^{-1}D$ (p. 350).[3] They finally give an example (pp. 351-2) of how to calculate how many possible combinations of rules of descent and 'marriage types' (of parents, sons, and daughters) exist in societies with four 'marriage types': the possibilities, they conclude, are six, and two of these six are said to be exemplified in known societies, viz. the Kariera and the Tarau.

<h1 style="text-align:center">VI</h1>

White devotes the main part of his book, *An Anatomy of Kinship* (1963), to the 'descriptions' of 'kinship structures that satisfy Kemeny–Snell–Thompson's axioms' (p. 32). He proposes only one conceptual modification: namely, to change the expression 'marriage type' in axiom 1 to that of 'clan', because 'marriage type' is 'not a concept to be found in the field notes of anthropologists or the thinking of members of the societies' (p. 32). 'Clan', instead, is defined as 'the largest group of persons in a tribe who follow the same preferential marriage rule with respect to other clans' (p. 33).[4]

The book is concerned with 'models of kinship systems with

[3] S = permutation matrix representing the marriage type of sons; D = permutation matrix representing the marriage type of daughters (Kemeny, Snell, and Thompson 1957: 346).
[4] It is not claimed, though, that this definition of the term is any more likely to be found in the field notes of anthropologists or in indigenous conceptions.

prescribed marriage' (as the title of the second chapter states). It presents an analysis of the mathematical definitions of a 'typology of societies', and an application of these models to 'known tribes,' viz. Kariera, Arunta, Murngin, Purum.

The typology presented in chapter II (p. 42) consists of:

 I *Bilateral marriage,* in which $W^2 = I$ and $WC = CW$;
 II *Matrilateral marriage,* in which $WC = CW$, but $W^2 \neq I$;
 III *Patrilateral marriage,* where $WC = CW^{-1}$, but $W^2 \neq I$;
 IV *Paired clans,* where $W^2 = I$, and $WC \neq CW$;
 V *Residual.*

In these definitions, W is the permutation matrix of side n (n = number of clans) and where 'each row of the matrix corresponds to a husband's clan, the wife's clan being identified with the column in which the number 1 appears in that row' (p. 35); and C is the permutation matrix in which '$C_{ij} = 1$ if fathers of clan i have children of clan j' (p. 35).

A major reformulation over the previous works consists in White's proposal of the matrices W and C instead of (as in the case of Kemeny, Snell, and Thompson) the matrices representing the transformation of parent's marriage type into son's and daughter's marriage type. This reformulation derives from the change of the concept of 'marriage type' for that of 'clan'.

A fundamental question for White is to answer 'what kind of relations can marry in a society specified by given C and W matrices' (p. 39). But prescriptive marriage types are for White only ideal types, limiting cases [in his book he succeeded in deriving ideal types only (pp. 148-9)], and the problem is not 'whether a tribe has a prescriptive as opposed to a preferential marriage system, but rather to what extent the tribe conforms to one or to some mixture of ideal types of prescribed marriage systems' (p. 148).

VII

In Courrège's 'Un modèle mathématique des structures élément-aires de parenté' (1965), the intention is:

to present, using the axiomatic method, a simple mathematical model that enables the study, for societies where the population is divided in discrete matrimonial classes, of the functioning

K

of the kinship system, i.e. the rules of marriage and descent expressed uniquely as a function of these classes (p. 248).

The mathematical model presented was built, Courrège says, to represent some of the kinship structures studied by Lévi-Strauss in *Les Structures élémentaires*, and specifically the Kariera, the Aranda, and the Murngin systems (p. 248), but it is also intended as a basis for classifying any kinship system with n matrimonial classes.

An *elementary structure of kinship* on a finite set S, says Courrège, is any triad (ω, μ, π) of permutations of S satisfying the following axiom:

$$(D) \quad \pi = \mu\omega \text{ (p. 253)}.$$

The ethnological meaning of S, ω, μ, π, is: the set S represents the set of classes of the society considered (and not, as White proposes, the set of individuals); the *conjugal function* ω represents a positive rule which 'prescribes' that a man of class $x(x \in S)$ shall choose his spouse in class $\omega(x)$; the *maternal function* μ represents a positive rule which 'prescribes' that all the children of a woman of class $x(x \in S)$ belong to class $\mu(x)$; and the *paternal function* π represents the same positive rule which 'prescribes' that all the children of a man of class $x(x \in S)$ belong to class $\pi(x)$.

Courrège goes on consistently giving mathematical expression to every possible analytical element in Lévi-Strauss's definition of elementary structures. An example of this is the 'condition for marriage between cross-cousins' (p. 261), where one learns that

> if a structure allows marriage with the matrilateral cross-cousin, in order for it to permit marriage with the patrilateral cross-cousin as well it is necessary and sufficient that it be a structure of restricted exchange.

This condition is expressed in Courrège's terminology by the following implication:

$$`\omega\mu = \mu\omega` \rightarrow `\omega\mu = \mu\omega^{-1} \leftrightarrow \omega^2 = \epsilon_8`$$

the verification of which is, he adds, 'immediate'.

One learns also that:

> for a set S of four elements, any regular structure allows marriage with the matrilateral cross-cousin (p. 261),

and that in such a structure patrilateral cross-cousin marriage is also allowed, so that for the 'structure' (ω_1, μ_1, π_1) and a set of four elements, $S = \{p, q, r, s\}$,

$$\omega_1 = \begin{pmatrix} p\ q\ r\ s \\ r\ s\ p\ q \end{pmatrix}, \mu_1 = \begin{pmatrix} p\ q\ r\ s \\ q\ p\ s\ r \end{pmatrix}, \pi_1 = \mu_1\,\omega_1 = \begin{pmatrix} p\ q\ r\ s \\ s\ r\ q\ p \end{pmatrix}$$

from which it may be 'verified' that

$$\omega^2 = \epsilon_s \text{ and } \omega_1\,\mu_1 = \mu_1\,\omega_1.$$

This structure (ω_1, μ_1, π_1) is to be called a 'Kariera structure' (p. 262).

He also gives formulations of this kind for a 'theoretical Murngin structure', 'structures of generalized exchange', and an 'Aranda structure'.

VIII

A common feature of all the articles examined is that none of their 'deductions' or 'interpretations' adds anything to the ethnographical facts known for any of the social structures analysed. Moreover, the 'deductions' or 'rules' that one is supposed to derive from Kemeny, Snell, and Thompson's exercises are facts readily available in the ethnographic accounts of any of the systems considered, and to know them is the first task of any anthropologist working on these topics. They are simply the basic data to consider when analysing a system anthropologically.

Thus one could hardly say that purpose (iii) of a translation, i.e. to be able to effect new developments by means of the translation applies to this case, at least from an anthropological point of view. Needless to say, purpose (i), viz. to communicate with a wider public, is out of the question, for what Leach says of White's book applies to all the works considered:

> The book is, in part, explicitly addressed to anthropologists (Preface), 99·9 per cent of whom could not read it even if they wanted to (*Man* 1964: 156).

Finally, what we have called purpose (ii) of a translation (to record and transmit information in a more synthetic form of expression) does not seem to be the case here either, for not only is it not the intention of the authors but one cannot see the point in transmitting the information in that way.

One consideration about this sort of formalization remains: sometimes, just by the effort of expressing a certain body of theory in a more formal language, the assumptions and premises involved become clearer or are made more explicit. With this possibility in mind, we shall analyse in the next section the axioms on which the works considered above are based.

IX

We need not take into account all seven of Kemeny, Snell, and Thompson's axioms, but just the first one and the variations on it in the rest of the articles on the subject.

The development of that axiom can be approached by way of Weil's statement that 'the individual men and women are divided into classes' (p. 278), and one of the conditions he posits: 'for any individual, man or woman, there is one and only one type of marriage he (or she) has the right to contract' (p. 279).

As we have seen above, Bush expresses this idea as follows:

> rather specific clans, moieties, generations, etc., are culturally defined for each man, his wife and his children. This permits us to distinguish a specific number of possible *marriage types* (p. 159).

Kemeny, Snell, and Thompson adopt this notion in their first axiom: 'each member of the society is assigned a marriage type' (p. 343).[5] White proposes instead to change the expression 'marriage type' to 'clan', because the former is not an anthropological concept. Therefore, he translates the first axiom into the following propositions:

> (1) the entire population of the society is divided into mutually exclusive groups, which we call *clans*;
> (2) there is a permanent rule fixing the single clan among whose women the men of a given clan must find their wives (p. 34).

Finally, Courrège deals with societies in which the population is divided into discrete matrimonial classes and where the rules of marriage and descent are expressed uniquely as a function of these classes (p. 248).

[5] They do not, however, provide any gloss on the operational interpretation of the qualifier that the clans are 'rather specific'.

We can summarize the different definitions of the types of society with which these authors are dealing as in *Table 11*. They

Table 11

Operational Concepts in Permutation Models

author	society divided into	units to be analysed
Weil (1949)	classes	marriage types
Bush [195?]	'rather specific' clans, moieties, generations	marriage types
Kemeny, Snell, & Thompson (1957)	[unstated]	marriage types
White (1963)	clans	clans
Courrège (1965)	classes	rules of marriage

are all supposed to be dealing with the mathematical interpretation of Lévi-Strauss's 'structures élémentaires', or at least, let us say, with societies in which the regulation of marriage is expressed as a positive rule. In other words, they are all trying to classify prescriptive systems, i.e. to classify societies that possess closed systems of classification.

X

In the light of the examples we have considered in this monograph, it is clear that what is meant by a 'prescriptive system' is a system in which the terminology constitutes a closed classification that implies a prescribed category of spouse.[6] The defining features of prescriptive systems are then:

   1 a lineal classification;
   2 a closed classification; and as an aspect of this,
   3 a necessary affinal relationship between categories that can be genealogically specified.

The defining features of these systems are not, therefore, a particular kind of 'mutually exclusive groupings', 'rather specific

---

[6] The technical distinction of a mode of alliance defined by the term 'prescription' seems to have been established by Hodson (1925).

clans', or 'marriage classes', but specific modes of social classification that define one category as the prescribed spouse, or what
Fison called in 1895 an ascriptive 'marital right' regarding certain
categories of persons.[7] From the point of view of an individual in a
society that possesses a prescriptive terminology, what counts in
the selection of the spouse is primarily the people classified in
terms of the prescribed category. Thus the Dieri marry a *nadada*,
and this prescription is related to their special kind of classification and not to actual discrete groups.

The fact that there exist in the societies considered actual
institutions or groups related to their social classification is
independent of the prescriptive character of their terminologies,
since these groupings or institutions vary from one society to
another. The 'sections' and 'subsections' of the Aranda have a
local reference and differ in any institutional respect from the
matrilineal totemic clans of the Dieri. The 'sections' or 'semi-
moieties' of the Mara, in turn, do not define their system of
classification and are not comparable with either the subsections
of the Aranda or the clans of the Dieri. The *ngaiva* of the Iatmül
do not in themselves define the Iatmül social classification, and
are not similar to the subsections of the Aranda, the clans of the
Dieri, or the 'semi-moieties' of the Mara.

XI

What then is a 'marriage type' and what is a 'clan', in the sense
White gives to the latter term? How to classify by means of
permutation models systems that possess a prescriptive terminology
and no 'classes'?

Concerning 'marriage types', there is no possible way to find an
empirical referent for such a conceptualization. Even in the case
of a two-line symmetric prescriptive terminology, concomitant
with four sections, as in the Kariera case, there exists only one
prescribed category, and the fact that the people denoted by that
category belong to different sections in consecutive genealogical
levels does not alter the definition of the terminology or the
prescription of a single category.

If we were to classify such a system by its terminology, it
would belong to the class of two-line symmetric prescriptive

[7] cf. Lévi-Strauss 1949: 9; 1967: 10; 1969: 8.

terminologies, which could in turn be subdivided into systems that possessed a concomitant set of sections[8] and systems that did not. But this subdivision would be composed of subclasses defined by a criterion different from the kind of terminology.

If, instead, we considered the existence of sections as the basic feature, we would create a classification from which systems with prescriptive terminologies of the same sort but without 'classes' would be excluded. In this latter case, the systems to classify would be fewer than in the first case.

While the terminological criterion cuts quite neatly between systems with or without prescriptive terminologies, the 'section' criterion has to deal with a heterogeneous set of systems, some of them with a set of sections concomitant with their relationship terminologies, some of them possessing sections not related to marriage alliances at all.

Still, our point here is that any prescriptive system possesses only one prescribed category, so that the concept of 'marriage types' is hard to visualize.

Regarding 'marriage classes', next, let us start by considering the definition of them in the second edition of Lévi-Strauss's *Les Structures élémentaires de la parenté*:

> I adopt a much broader definition of marriage class; i.e. class is defined unequivocally, such that the members of the class have certain marriage constraints which are different from those imposed on the members of another class (1967: 310).

If we adopt this definition, the term becomes confused with that of 'marriage type' as used by Weil, Bush, and Kemeny, Snell, and Thompson, and with that of 'clan' as used by White.

In this case one cannot do less than point out that Weil's use of both terms, viz. 'class' and 'marriage type', becomes redundant. But that could be just Weil's problem and we could still consider the relevance of the concept. In connection with this point, let us consider first a modification Sperber suggests for the formalization of the 'Kariera structure' (Sperber 1968: 225-6). He considers an example in which there are two hypothetical systems, E and F, the models of which are:

$$E = \{A \ B\} \ P_e = \begin{Bmatrix} A \ B \\ A \ B \end{Bmatrix} \ m_e = \begin{Bmatrix} A \ B \\ B \ A \end{Bmatrix} \ f_e = \begin{Bmatrix} A \ B \\ B \ A \end{Bmatrix}$$

[8] Including exogamous moieties in correspondence with a two-line terminology.

E is a system of two exogamous patrilineal classes (moieties).

$$F = \{X\ Y\}\ P_{\mathfrak{f}} = \begin{Bmatrix} X\ Y \\ Y\ X \end{Bmatrix}\ m_{\mathfrak{f}} = \begin{Bmatrix} X\ Y \\ X\ Y \end{Bmatrix}\ f_{\mathfrak{f}} = \begin{Bmatrix} X\ Y \\ X\ Y \end{Bmatrix}$$

F is a system of exogamous matrilineal moieties.

One is able to construct a system G, which is the product of E and F:

$$\begin{aligned}
G &= E \times F &&= \{AX\ AY\ BX\ BY\} \\
p_{\mathrm{g}} &= p_{\mathrm{e}} \times p_{\mathfrak{f}} &&= \begin{Bmatrix} AX\ AY\ BX\ BY \\ AY\ AX\ BY\ BX \end{Bmatrix} \\
m_{\mathrm{g}} &= m_{\mathrm{e}} \times m_{\mathfrak{f}} &&= \begin{Bmatrix} AX\ AY\ BX\ BY \\ BX\ BY\ AX\ AY \end{Bmatrix} \\
f_{\mathrm{g}} &= f_{\mathrm{e}} \times f_{\mathfrak{f}} &&= \begin{Bmatrix} AX\ AY\ BX\ BY \\ BY\ BX\ AY\ AX \end{Bmatrix}
\end{aligned}$$

The model thus obtained is a representation of the Kariera system, Sperber says, but he adds that the Kariera do not possess actual matrilineal moieties, so the system could be derived from E and, instead of F (exogamous matrilineal moieties), a rule of alternation of generations, which he calls H and represents as follows:

$$H = \{1\ 2\}\ p_{\mathrm{h}} = \begin{Bmatrix} 1\ 2 \\ 2\ 1 \end{Bmatrix}\ m_{\mathrm{h}} = \begin{Bmatrix} 1\ 2 \\ 2\ 1 \end{Bmatrix}\ f_{\mathrm{h}} = \begin{Bmatrix} 1\ 2 \\ 1\ 2 \end{Bmatrix}$$

But if one rejects the first formulation he gives, because it is not convenient to introduce in the models 'potential matrilineal moieties', what is the ground for Lévi-Strauss's 'marriage classes', which also are a 'conceptual tool' and do not always have an actual empirical referent?

Another problem in the reformulation presented by Sperber is that 'alternation of generations' is not a 'rule', but a distinctive feature (itself the resultant of certain principles, cf. chapter 6) of a type of terminology, in the case of a four-line symmetric prescriptive terminology, or a rule superimposed on a two-line symmetric prescriptive terminology. It does not seem convenient, therefore, to introduce it into the models.

XII

There is a further consideration on the validity of permutation models that derives from our definition of prescriptive terminologies. The question is whether the models would apply if the symbols A, B, ... N, in the models were redefined as the component lines of prescriptive terminologies; i.e. in which the lines corresponded to the arrangements of the terms as they were put into practical effect by the people who actually employed these terminologies.

Let us consider the case of symmetric prescriptive terminologies. In the case of one of these terminologies composed of two lines, we could consider these two lines as A and B. A would be the set of terms that form a line; B the set of terms that form the opposite line.

The functions m, f, and w employed in the permutation models would represent the relationship between categories in the terminology according to (i) line, and (ii) prescribed category.

Thus m would represent the relationship between categories specified as M (mother) and C (children); f, the relationship between categories specified as F (father) and C (children), and w, the relationship between categories specified as H (husband) and W (wife).

A system E, defined by a two-matriline prescriptive terminology, would be represented as follows:[9]

$$E \ = \{A\ B\}$$
$$m_\mathrm{e} \ = \begin{Bmatrix} A\ B \\ A\ B \end{Bmatrix}$$
$$f_\mathrm{e} \ = \begin{Bmatrix} A\ B \\ B\ A \end{Bmatrix}$$
$$w_\mathrm{e} \ = \begin{Bmatrix} A\ B \\ B\ A \end{Bmatrix}$$

This system does not seem to present any inconvenience and the logic seems to be the same as when considering the symbols A, B ... N, representing actual groupings in a 'two-section system'.

Let us consider now the case of a four-line prescriptive terminology. We will take the Dieri as our example. A system S, thus, will be composed of A, B, C, D, each of the symbols representing a matriline. Lines A and B correspond to one division of the terminology and have their prescribed categories in C and D, which compose the opposite division. The prescribed categories for C and D, then, belong to A and B.

[9] We are considering a terminology composed of matrilines for the sake of continuity with our next example.

The system S can be represented as follows:

$$S = \{A\ B\ C\ D\}$$

Function m is represented as:

$$m_{\mathrm{S}} = \begin{Bmatrix} A\ B\ C\ D \\ A\ B\ C\ D \end{Bmatrix}$$

That is to say, the categories specified as C (children) belong to the same line as the categories specified as M (mother).

Function f is represented as:

$$f = \begin{Bmatrix} A_1\ A_2\ B_1\ B_2\ C_1\ C_2\ D_1\ D_2 \\ C_2\ D_1\ D_2\ C_1\ A_2\ B_1\ B_2\ A_1 \end{Bmatrix}$$

in which the subindices 1 and 2 stand for different genealogical levels: 1 for levels I, III, and V, and 2 for levels II and IV.

But, even without going any further, it can be seen that m and f do not represent permutations; and there is no way to transform a permutation composed of A, B, C, and D into f_{S} by means of a rule of alternation of genealogical levels such as the rule H proposed by Sperber for the Kariera.

Still, one could consider the four lines (A, B, C, D) and the alternating levels 1 and 2 and represent the Dieri terminology as:

$$S = \{A_1\ A_2\ B_1\ B_2\ C_1\ C_2\ D_1\ D_2\}$$

$$m_{\mathrm{S}} = \begin{Bmatrix} A_1\ A_2\ B_1\ B_2\ C_1\ C_2\ D_1\ D_2 \\ A_2\ A_1\ B_2\ B_1\ C_2\ C_1\ D_2\ D_1 \end{Bmatrix}$$

$$f_{\mathrm{S}} = \begin{Bmatrix} A_1\ A_2\ B_1\ B_2\ C_1\ C_2\ D_1\ D_2 \\ C_2\ D_1\ D_2\ C_1\ B_2\ A_1\ A_2\ B_1 \end{Bmatrix}$$

$$w_{\mathrm{S}} = \begin{Bmatrix} A_1\ A_2\ B_1\ B_2\ C_1\ C_2\ D_1\ D_2 \\ D_1\ C_2\ C_1\ D_2\ B_1\ A_2\ A_1\ B_2 \end{Bmatrix}$$

In this representation of a four-matriline symmetric prescriptive terminology:

(i) there is no way of composing this system deductively from any previous system (cf. Sperber 1967: 224-6), not even by applying a rule H; and

(ii) setting aside the deductibility of the model, as a representation of the Dieri terminology, it does not express anything more clearly or more revealingly than a diagram such as in *Figure 12* (p. 65). Moreover, in order to state m_{S}, f_{S}, and w_{S}, one has to construct the diagram first.

From this last point, one wonders, therefore, whether it would not be better to represent the terminologies in the usual and considerably simpler form of a diagram. In this connection, Lévi-Strauss states:

> I fail to see why an algebraic treatment of, let us say, symbols for marriage rules, could not teach us, when aptly manipulated, something about the way a given marriage system actually works, and bring out properties not immediately apparent at the empirical level (1960b: 53).

After considering the works devoted to the algebraical treatment of prescriptive systems, we fail to see, instead, what are the advantages of such a treatment and what 'properties not immediately apparent at the empirical level' they bring out.

Chapter Eight

Conclusions

I

The problems in *Les Structures élémentaires de la parenté* start with the very definition of what it is about. Although the presentation of the elementary–complex typology in the first edition of the book was quite clear in stating the sort of closed systems Lévi-Strauss was concerned with, later publications and the author's preface to the second edition made the question obscure. We have had to demonstrate (chapter 3) that Leach is right in saying that 'as time goes on, it becomes increasingly difficult to understand just what Lévi-Strauss really means by "elementary structures"' (Leach 1969a: 105).

But if we take 'elementary structures' to be literally what Lévi-Strauss's definition in the first edition of the book quite specifically states, then it is still possible to search for the reason for their existence and their connection with other factors as explained by Lévi-Strauss. The 'incest taboo' is given both as the logical counterpart and as the genetical antecedent of 'elementary structures'. We have shown in chapter 1 not only that both these connections are fallacious, but that the very concept of incest prohibitions and its relations with the concepts of 'nature' and 'culture' are ill defined in Lévi-Strauss's book.

Independently of their logical counterparts and their genetical antecedents, elementary structures can still be considered as Lévi-Strauss's version of prescriptive systems, a class of society long recognized in the literature. As such they are divided in *Les Structures élémentaires* into two types defined by restricted and generalized exchange. Lévi-Strauss relates the two types to an independent variable, viz. 'regime', and this postulate constitutes the only falsifiable hypothesis for an explanation of elementary

structures in the entire book. But one of the examples that Lévi-
Strauss himself presents, namely the Aranda case, shows, when
analysed correctly, that the hypothesis is false (chapter 2).

According to Lévi-Strauss, there are evolutionary connections
among different types of elementary structures. One of them
establishes the precedence of generalized exchange over restricted
exchange and is exemplified by the Dieri system, among others.
In considering the ethnographical literature on the Dieri (chapter
4), we have been able to demonstrate, once more, that, as in the
case of the Wikmunkan (cf. Needham 1962b), the precedence of
generalized exchange over restricted exchange cannot be established
by reference to the Dieri case (any more than it has yet been
shown by any other), and, in addition, that the Dieri system
actually bears almost no resemblance to the description and interpretation published by Lévi-Strauss.

Lévi-Strauss proposes also that systems of 'patrilateral' marriage
are the basis for alternating systems. In the course of our monograph we have dealt with four systems of the alternating type.
None of them can be considered as a confirmation of Lévi-Strauss's
proposition, not even the Mara case, which Lévi-Strauss presents
as conclusive evidence of his ideas (chapter 6).

In this last respect, the Iatmül case served to show that the
alternation of terms by genealogical level is not confined to
symmetric systems, and that Lèvi-Strauss's definition of 'prescription' and 'preference' makes the application of his concept
of 'elementary structures' impossible.

Although Lévi-Strauss believes that an algebraic treatment of
prescriptive systems can 'bring out properties not immediately
apparent at the empirical level' (1960b: 53), and consequently
adds an appendix by a mathematician applying permutation models
to some of his cases, we have shown (chapter 7) that mathematical
techniques of the kind are not the best way of dealing with such
systems. The application of permutation models seems so far not
to be an ideal technique either to describe prescriptive systems
or to explain them.

II

Les Structures élémentaires de la parenté thus arranges some of the
most interesting ideas conceived by Lévi-Strauss's predecessors

in many decades of social anthropology, but in a rhetorical, ill-ordered, and contradictory scheme. It is built upon defective reasoning combined with deficient or mistaken reports of the ethnographical facts.

Our findings about the precariousness of Lévi-Strauss's empirical analyses, and his carelessness when dealing with concepts, reaffirm what Needham expressed about *Les Structures élémentaires* in 1962:

> in a number of places . . . I have had to observe that Professor Lévi-Strauss has sometimes neglected theoretical predecessors and failed to use important ethnographic sources, that he has incorrectly analysed certain systems and wrongly supposed diagnostic signs of others, and that he has even ascribed to one society facts relating to another (1962c: 170, n. 10).

They also confirm what Leach has to say when discussing Lévi-Strauss's use of the Kachin data: 'Lévi-Strauss, as always, has everything back to front' (Leach 1969b: 284). In this connection we have found that Revel's fears regarding *Les Structures élementaires* were justified:

> when one sees how sociologists talk about societies that we know, it inspires the greatest distrust of what they say about those that we do not know (Revel 1957: 145).

Lévi-Strauss's book is written in a style that leads the reader to think that he is unable to grasp the deep, real meaning of the work, because of its highly technical level. This impression comes, in fact, mainly from the use of more than one term to designate the same concept (e.g. 'restricted' and 'direct' designate the same sort of exchange), from the development of 'deductions' that have neither empirical support nor logical consistency, and from reifications by which Nature and Culture discourse with each other or systems of generalized exchange are afflicted by a 'patrilateral nostalgia' (1949: 590).

As far as the style is concerned, there is at least a hope that Lévi-Strauss would now wish to rectify it, because he himself has said that twenty years after writing the book, 'the expression [seems] old-fashioned'. But there would be no hope, on the other hand, that Lévi-Strauss would reconsider any other aspect of the work, because in this respect, and also twenty years after he wrote it, he rejects 'not one part of the theoretical inspiration or of the method, nor any of the principles of interpretation' (1967: xiii).

III

The objection might be raised that the critique presented here is irrelevant or misguided because it is directed mainly to Lévi-Strauss's empirical analyses, whereas his approach is 'en effet, très lointaine du concret' (Simonis 1968: 127). Lévi-Strauss has certainly affirmed, since 1965 at least, that he is interested in models and not in empirical reality (1965: 17; 1967: 58 n. 20).

We have dealt elsewhere (Korn 1969a) with Lévi-Strauss's conception of 'model' and with that striking feature which he ascribes to 'structures' by which they are at the same time 'the content itself' (Lévi-Strauss 1960a: 3) yet also 'not related to empirical reality' (1958b: 305). But quite apart from his own definition of 'model' and his peculiar conception of 'structure', what is the place of empirical test in his theory? Why does he need to refer at all to the Kariera, the Aranda, the Dieri, the Mara, and the rest, if he is not concerned with their actual systems as forms of collective ideation and social life?

> If a structure can be seen, it will be not at the earlier, empirical level, but at a deeper one, previously neglected; that of those unconscious categories which we may hope to reach, by bringing together domains which at first sight appear disconnected to the observer: on the one hand, the social system as it actually works, and on the other, the manner in which, through their myths, their ritual and their religious representations, men try to hide or justify the discrepancies between their society and the ideal image of it which they habour (1960b: 53).

But what if one neglects, as he does, that 'earlier empirical level'? How does one discover how a social system 'actually works' if one is 'not concerned with empirical reality'? What if one describes a social structure that does not belong to the people one is supposed to be talking about? Whose 'unconscious' categories is one then hoping to reach? And what does it mean that one is concerned with models and not with empirical reality? Models of what?

The study of marriage rules implies at least three levels of analysis: (1) explicit rules as expressed by the members of a society; (2) rules inferred from the statistical frequency of marriages between certain categories; (3) rules implied by the different arrangements of relationship terms. The rules involved in the two first levels may or may not coincide with those deriving from the third, as we have seen particularly in the Iatmül case. The extent of coincidence between the three levels derives from the degree of consistency between behaviour and ideology, between what people do and what people think ought to be done, between what people think ought to be done and the principles by which they are classified into categories and groups. The models with which Lévi-Strauss claims to be concerned are presumably the representation of the different combinations of these principles. Unless the actual systems are correctly described, one can never be sure what principles are involved in social classification, which of the logical combinations of these principles are empirical, and whether a hypothesis concerning these combinations is confirmed or refuted by the facts.

Any search for 'unconscious categories' has inevitably to begin and end with empirical analysis. And if a system of social classification, as expressed in a relationship terminology, is what Lévi-Strauss means by 'unconscious model', then he needs to make sure that what he is describing is in fact the 'unconscious model' of the society he is studying and not his own.

IV

Any intellectual product that is meant to be an explanation of something is susceptible of evaluation by means of the criteria of logical consistency and testability. There are no mysteries about 'methods'. There are ideas, concepts, definitions, hypotheses, and empirical proofs. In this respect we cannot agree with Scholte's statement that 'one cannot criticize Lévi-Strauss in terms of criteria to which his work *is not meant to conform*' (Scholte 1970: 117; original emphasis). There are no special criteria of evaluation for particular works. Lévi-Strauss's monograph is not immune to the demands of logic and empirical test; or, if it is, then it has no claim to any scientific status. If Lévi-Strauss himself reaffirms the theoretical inspiration, the method, and the principles of interpretation of his own book – which is meant, after all, to be an introduction to a general theory – we do not see why it should be treated differently from any other scientific attempt.

Maybury-Lewis, writing of Lévi-Strauss's empirical analyses in *The Savage Mind*, says that 'when he comes down from the clouds and deals with specific cases, he is often trivial or just plain wrong'. But, he maintains, 'it is unreasonable to expect anybody to be always theoretically brilliant, or even regularly right' (Maybury-Lewis 1970: 139). We have indeed been able to demonstrate the triviality or the wrongness of certain analyses in *Les Structures élémentaires*, but we have not found it possible to illustrate any respects in which it is theoretically brilliant or even regularly right. In fact, the outcome of our own experience when dealing with Lévi-Strauss's specific cases is that when he departs from the work of his predecessors he is usually mistaken. It is a problem, rather, to account for the renown of a theoretician who is unimpressive as an analyst and whose theories, which are seldom original, are regularly refuted by the facts.

L

Appendix

Comparative Table of Dieri
Terms of Relationship

The following list of different sets of terms considers only the
accounts of the Dieri relationship terminology based on ethnographic research. We do not include in this Appendix either
Howitt's 1904 list or Elkin's 1931 list, which can both be found
in the course of chapter 4 (*Tables 4* and *5* respectively). The lists
are presented in chronological order; the terms have been arranged
mainly by genealogical level. In the reports of Wettenfel, Vogelsang
(8), and Berndt, $j = y$.

1. Meissel (in Taplin 1871)
   1. *ngaperi*   F
   2. *ngandri*   M

2. Gason (in Woods 1879: 294-303)
   1. *adada*   grandfather
   2. *kunninnie*   grandmother
   3. *apinie*   F
   4. *andrie*   M
   5. *kaka*   uncle
   6. *thuroo*   father-in-law
   7. *piyara*   mother-in-law
   8. *niehie*   eB
   9. *kakoo*   eZ
   10. *athata*   yB, yZ
   11. *noa*   H, W
   12. *athamoora*   S, D (so called by the father)
   13. *athanie*   S, D (so called by the mother)
   14. *thidnara*   nephew

15. *pirraooroo*   paramour
16. *pinaroo*   old man
17. *munkara*   girl on marriage

3. Gason (in Howitt 1891: 45-9)
    1. *apiri*   F
    2. *apiri wauka*   FB, MZH, M's *pirauru*
    3. *andri*   M
    4. *andri wauka*   MZ, FBW, F's *pirauru*
    5. *kaka*   MB
    6. *niehie*   eB, FBeS, MZeS, F's *pirauru*'s eS
    7. *kakoo*   eZ, FBeD, MZeD, F's *pirauru*'s eD
    8. *athata*   yB, yZ, FByS, FByD, MZyS, MZyD, F's *pirauru*'s yS
    9. *kummie*   FZS, FZD, MBS, MBD
    10. *noa*   H, W
    11. *noa wauka*   HB, ZH, WZ, BW
    12. *piraooroo*   accessory H, accessory W
    13. *kareti*   WB
    14. *kamari*   HZ
    15. *athamoora*   S, BS, WZS (m.s.)
    16. *athani*   S (w.s.)
    17. *athani wauka*   ZS, HBS (w.s.)

4. Vogelsang (in Howitt 1891: 45-9)
    1. *appiri*   F, FB, MZH
    2. *ngandri*   M, FBW
    3. *ngandri wauka*   MZ
    4. *kaka*   MB, FZH
    5. *papa*   FZ, MBW
    6. *negi*   eB, FBeS, MZeS, F's *pirauru*'s eS
    7. *kakoo*   eZ, FBeD, MZeD, F's *pirauru*'s eD
    8. *ngatata*   yB, yZ, FByS, FByD, MZyS, MZyD, F's *pirauru*'s yS and yD
    9. *kami*   FZS, FZD, MBS, MBD
    10. *noa*   H, W, WZ, BW
    11. *kareti*   WB
    12. *kamari*   HZ
    13. *ngatamura*   S, BS, WZS (m.s.)
    14. *ngatani*   S, ZS, HBS
    15. *tinara*   ZS

5. Meyer (in Howitt 1891: 45-9)

1.	*aperi*	F
2.	*aperi waka*	MZH
3.	*andri*	M
4.	*andri waka*	FBW
5.	*kaka*	MB, FZH
6.	*papa*	FZ, MBW
7.	*negi*	eB, FBeS, MZeS, F's *pirauru*'s S
8.	*kaku*	eZ, FBeD, MZeD, F's *pirauru*'s D
9.	*ngatata*	yB, yZ, FByS, FByD, F's *pirauru*'s yS and yD, MZyS, MZyD
10.	*kami*	FZS, MBS, FZD, MBD
11.	*noa*	H, W
12.	*yimari*	ZH (w.s.), WZ
13.	*kamari*	BW (m.s.), HZ
14.	*nginyaru*	accessory husband
15.	*piranguru*	accessory wife
16.	*kadi*	WB
17.	*ngata mùra*	S, BS, WZS (m.s.), BS (w.s.)
18.	*ngatani*	S, ZS, HBS (w.s.)

6. Flierl (in Howitt 1891: 45-9)

1.	*aperi*	F
2.	*aperi waka*	FB
3.	*andri*	M
4.	*andri waka*	MZ, FBW, F's *pirauru*
5.	*kaka*	MB, FZH
6.	*papa*	FZ, MBW
7.	*negi*	eB, FBeS, MZeS, F's *pirauru*'s eS
8.	*kaku*	eZ, FBeD, MZeD, F's *pirauru*'s eD
9.	*ngatata*	yB, yZ, FByS, FByD, MZyS, MZyD, F's *pirauru*'s yS and yD
10.	*kami*	FZS, FZD, MBS, MBD
11.	*noa*	H, W
12.	*noa waka*	HB, ZH, WZ
13.	*yimari*	HB, ZH, WZ
14.	*kamari*	BW (m.s.), HZ
15.	*kadi*	WB
16.	*pirauru*	accessory husband
17.	*nginyaru*	accessory wife

18. *ngata mùra*   S, BS, WZS (m.s.)
19. *ngatani*   S, ZS, HBS
20. *tidnara*   ZS

7. Wettenfel (in Planert 1908: 688-96)
    1. *ngaperi*   F
    2. *ngapi-ni*   own F
    3. *ngandri*   M
    4. *neji*   eB
    5. *ngatata*   yB
    6. *noa*   spouse
    7. *ngatamura*   S
    8. *waka-kupa*   yS

8. Vogelsang (in Berndt and Vogelsang 1941: 3-6)
    1. *'naperi*   F
    2. *'nandri*   M
    3. *'neje*   eB
    4. *'kaku*   eZ
    5. *'noa*   H, W

9. Berndt (1953: 171-93)
    1. *jengu*   FFZ, SD
    2. *gami*   FMB, WFF, MBS, ZSS, MBD, FM,
                       ZSD, MMBSDH
    3. *gaga*   MB
    4. *niji*   eB
    5. *nadada*   eBW
    6. *didnara*   ZS, FMBS
    7. *daru*   FMBS, WF
    8. *gagu*   MMBSD

Bibliography

BATESON, G.
  1932a Social Structure of the Iatmül People of the Sepik River. *Oceania*, **2**: 246-89.
  1932b Social Structure of the Iatmül People of the Sepik River. *Oceania*, **2**: 401-51.
B[ATESON], G.
  1935 Music in New Guinea. *The Eagle*: A magazine supported by the Members of St John's College (Cambridge, CUP), **48**: 158-70.
BATESON, G.
  1936 *Naven*. Cambridge: Cambridge University Press.
BERNDT, R. M.
  1953 A Day in the Life of a Dieri Man before Alien Contact. *Anthropos*, **47**: 170-201.
BERNDT, R. M., and BERNDT, C.
  1939 Notes on the Dieri Tribe of South Australia. *Transactions of the Royal Society of South Australia*, **63**: 2.
  1941 Initiation of Native Doctors, Dieri Tribe of South Australia. *Records of the South Australian Museum*, **6**: 376-7.
BERNDT, R. M. and VOGELSANG, T.
  1941 Comparative Vocabularies of the Ngadjuri and Dieri Tribes, South Australia. *Transactions of the Royal Society of South Australia*, **65**: 3-10.
BOUDON, R.
  1968 *A quoi sert la notion de 'structure'? Essai sur la signification de la notion de structure dans les sciences humaines*. Paris: Gallimard.
BROUGH SMYTH, R.
  1878 *Aborigines of Victoria*. 2 vols. London: Trübner.

BUSH, R.
1963   An Algebraic Treatment of Rules of Marriage and Descent. In White 1963: 159-72.

COURRÈGE, PH.
1965   Un modèle mathématique des structures élémentaires de parenté. *L'Homme,* **5**: 248-90.

DOUGLAS, M.
1967   The Meaning of Myth, with special reference to 'La Geste d'Asdiwal'. In Leach 1967: 49-70.

DUCROT, O., *et al.*
1968   *Qu'est-ce que le structuralisme?* Paris: Editions du Seuil.

DUMONT, L.
1957   *Hierarchy and Marriage Alliance in South Indian Kinship.* (Occasional Papers of the Royal Anthropological Institute, no. 12). London: Royal Anthropological Institute.
1964   Marriage in India: the present state of the question. *Contributions to Indian Sociology,* no. 7: 77-98.
1966   Descent or Intermarriage? A Relational View of Australian Section Systems. *Southwestern Journal of Anthropology,* **22**: 231-50.

DURKHEIM, E.
1897   Review of Kohler, *Zur Urgeschichte der Ehe. Année Sociologique,* **1**: 306-19.
1898   La prohibition de l'inceste et ses origines. *Année Sociologique,* **1**: 1-70.
1902   Sur le totémisme. *Année Sociologique,* **5**: 82-121.

ELKIN, A. P.
1931   The Dieri Kinship System. *Journal of the Royal Anthropological Institute,* **61**: 493-8.
1934   Cult-totemism and Mythology in Northern South Australia. *Oceania,* **5**: 171-92.
1937   Beliefs and Practices connected with Death in North-Eastern and Western South Australia. *Oceania,* **7**: 275-99.
1938a   Kinship in South Australia. *Oceania,* **9**: 41-78.
1938b   Review of Bateson 1936. *Oceania,* **8**: 373-5.
1964   *The Australian Aborigines.* [First edition, 1938.] Sydney: Angus and Robertson.

FISON, L.
1893   Group Marriage and Relationship. *Report of the Australasian Association for the Advancement of Science,* Sydney, **4**: 688-97.
1895   The Classificatory System of Relationship. *Journal of the Anthropological Institute,* **24**: 360-71.

FISON, L., and HOWITT, A. W.
   1880   *Kamilaroi and Kurnai.* Melbourne: Robertson.
FORGE, A.
   1971   Marriage and Exchange in the Sepik. Chapter 5 in
           Rethinking Kinship and Marriage, ed. R. Needham. ASA
           Monograph no. 11. London: Tavistock Publications.
FOX, R.
   1967   *Kinship and Marriage.* Harmondsworth, Middx.: Penguin
           Books.
   1969   Crow–Omaha System and the Elementary–Complex
           Continuum: Problems for Research. In Nutini, H. G., and
           Buchler, I. (eds.) *Essays in Social Anthropology: In Honor
           of Claude Lévi-Strauss.*
FRAZER, J. G.
   1910   *Totemism and Exogamy.* London: Macmillan.
FRY, H. K.
   1931   A Table showing the Class Relations of the Aranda.
           Transactions of the Royal Society of South Australia, **55**:
           12-19.
   1934   Kinship and Descent among the Australian Aborigines.
           Transactions of the Royal Society of South Australia, **58**:
           14-21.
   1950   Aboriginal Social Systems. *Transactions of the Royal
           Society of South Australia,* **73**: 282-94.
   1957   Concerning Aboriginal Marriage and Kinship. *Trans-
           actions of the Royal Society of South Australia,* **80**: 1-16.
GASON, S.
   1874   *The Dieyerie Tribe of Australian Aborigines, their Manners
           and Customs.* Adelaide.
   1888   Note on the Dieyerie Tribe of South Australia. *Journal of
           the Anthropological Institute,* **17**: 185-6.
   1899   The Dieyerie Tribe, South Australia. *Journal of the
           Anthropological Institute,* **18**: 94-5.
GATTI, G.
   1930   *La Lingua Dieri, Contributo alla Cognoscenza delle Lingue
           Australiane.* Roma: Scuola Salesiana del Libro.
GREENWAY, J.
   1963   *Bibliography of the Australian Aborigines and the Native
           Peoples of Torres Strait to 1959.* London: Angus and
           Robertson.
HAYES, E. N., and HAYES, T. (eds.)
   1970   *Claude Lévi-Strauss: The Anthropologist as Hero.* Cam-
           bridge, Massachusetts: The MIT Press.

HOCART, A. M.
1933   Arunta Language: Strehlow v. Spencer and Gillen. *Man*, 33: 96.
1937   Kinship Systems. *Anthropos*, **38**: 345-51.

HODSON, T. C.
1925   Notes on the Marriage of Cousins in India. *Man in India*, 5: 163-75.

HOWITT, A. W.
1878   Notes on the Aborigines of Cooper's Creek. In Brough Smyth 1878, 2, Appendix D: 300-9.
1883   Notes on the Australian Class System. *Journal of the Anthropological Institute*, **12**: 496-512.
1884a   Appendix II, in Palmer 1884.
1884b   On Some Australian Ceremonies of Initiation. *Journal of the Anthropological Institute*, **13**: 432-59.
1888   Further Notes on the Australian Classes. *Journal of the Anthropological Institute*, **18**: 31-67.
1890   Note as to Descent in the Dieri Tribe. *Journal of the Anthropological Institute*, **10**: 90.
1891   The Dieri and other Kindred Tribes of Central Australia. *Journal of the Anthropological Institute*, **20**: 30-104.
1904   *The Native Tribes of South-East Australia.* London: Macmillan.
1906a   The Native Tribes of South-East Australia. *Folk-lore*, **17**: 107-10.
1906b   The Native Tribes of South-East Australia. *Folk-lore*, **17**: 174-89.
1907a   The Native Tribes of South-East Australia. *Folk-lore*, **18**: 166-86.
1907b   The Native Tribes of South-East Australia. *Journal of the Anthropological Institute*, **37**: 268-78.

HOWITT, A. W., and SIEBERT, O.
1904   Legends of the Dieri and Kindred Tribes of Central Australia. *Journal of the Anthropological Institute*, **34**: 100-29.

JOSSELIN DE JONG, J. P. B. DE
1952   *Lévi-Strauss's Theory of Kinship and Marriage.* Leiden: Brill.

KEMENY, J. G., SNELL, J. L., and THOMPSON, G. L.
1957   *Introduction to Finite Mathematics.* Englewood Cliffs, N. J.: Prentice-Hall.

KORN, F.
1969a   The Use of the Term 'Model' in some of Lévi-Strauss's

M

Works. *Bijdragen tot de Taal-, Land- en Volkenkunde*, **125**: 1-11.

1969b   The Logic of Some Concepts in Lévi-Strauss. *American Anthropologist*, **71**: 70-1.

1969c   Review of Boudon 1968. *Critica* (Mexico), **7**.

1970a   Terminology and 'Structure': The Dieri Case. *Bijdragen tot de Taal-, Land- en Volkenkunde*, **127**: 39-81.

1970b   A Question of Preferences: The Iatmül Case. In Needham 1971a: 99-132.

KORN, F., and NEEDHAM, R.

1969   *Lévi-Strauss on the Elementary Structures of Kinship: A Concordance to Pagination*. London: Royal Anthropological Institute.

1970   Permutation Models and Prescriptive Systems: The Tarau Case. *Man*, n.s., **5**: 393-420.

KROEBER, A. L.

1909   Classificatory Systems of Relationship. *Journal of the Royal Anthropological Institute*, **39**: 77-84.

1953   (ed.) *Anthropology Today*. Chicago: University of Chicago Press.

KRUYT, A. C.

1922   De Soembaneezen. *Bijdragen tot de Taal-, Land- en Volkenkunde van Nederlandsch-Indië*, **77**: 466-608.

LANE, B., and LANE, R.

1962   Implicit Double Descent in South Australia and the North-Eastern New Hebrides. *Ethnology*, **1**: 46-52.

LANG, A.

1902   The Origin of Totem Names and Beliefs. *Folk-lore*, **13**: 347-97.

1903   *Social Origins*. London: Longmans, Green.

1905a   *The Secret of the Totem*. London: Longmans, Green.

1905b   All-fathers in Australia. *Folk-lore*, **16**: 222-5.

1906   Mr Howitt's Native Tribes of South-East Australia: A Correction. *Man*, **6**: 122.

1907   The Native Tribes of South-East Australia: a Reply to Dr Howitt. *Man*, **7**: 102-4.

1909   Mr Gason and Dieri Totemism. *Man*, **9**: 52-3.

1911   Lord Avebury on Marriage, Totemism and Religion. *Folk-lore*, **22**: 402-25.

LAYARD, J.

1942   *Stone Men of Malekula*. London: Chatto and Windus.

LEACH, E.

1954   *Political Systems of Highland Burma*. London: Bell.

1960   The Sinhalese of the Dry Zone of Northern Ceylon. In
            Murdock 1960: 116-26.
1961   *Rethinking Anthropology*. London: Athlone Press.
1967a   (ed.) *The Structural Study of Myth and Totemism*. (ASA
            Monographs 5.) London: Tavistock Publications.
1967b   Introduction in Leach 1967a: vii-xix.
1969a   *Lévi-Strauss*. London: Collins.
1969b   'Kachin' and 'Haka Chin': A Rejoinder to Lévi-Strauss.
            Man, 4: 277-85.

LEONHARDI, M. VON
1909   Der Mura und die Mura-Mura der Dieri. *Anthrops*, 4:
            1065-8.

LÉVI-STRAUSS, C.
1949   *Les Structures élémentaires de la parenté*. Paris: Presses
            Universitaires de France.
1953   Social Structure. In Kroeber (ed.) 1953: 524-53.
1955   Les Structures élémentaires de la parenté. *La Progenèse*,
            105-10.
1958   *Anthropologie Structurale*. Paris: Plon.
1960a   La structure et la forme, réflexions sur un ouvrage de
            Vladimir Propp. *Cahiers de l'Institut de Sciences Econ-
            omiques et Appliqueés*, no. 99, Paris.
1960b   On Manipulated Sociological Models. *Bijdragen tot de
            Taal-, Land- en Volkenkunde*, 16: 45-54.
1962a   *Le Totémisme aujourd'hui*. Paris: Presses Universitaires de
            France.
1962b   *La Pensée sauvage*. Paris: Plon.
1963a   Réponses à quelques questions. *Esprit*, no. 322: 628-53.
1963b   *Totemism*. Translated by Rodney Needham. Boston:
            Beacon Press; London: Merlin.
1963c   *Structural Anthropology*. Translated by Claire Jacobson
            and Brooke Grundfest Schoepf. New York: Basic Books.
1965   The Future of Kinship Studies. *Proceedings of the Royal
            Anthropological Institute*: 13-21.
1966a   Anthropology: Its Achievements and Future. *Current
            Anthropology*, 7: 124-7.
1966b   *The Savage Mind*. Chicago: University of Chicago
            Press.
1967   *Les Structures élémentaires de la parenté*. 2nd edition, rev.
            Paris and The Hague: Mouton.
1969   *The Elementary Structures of Kinship*. Edited by Rodney
            Needham, translated by J. H. Bell, J. R. von Sturmer, and
            R. Needham. London: Eyre and Spottiswoode.

LIENHARDT, G.
1964   *Social Anthropology*. London: Oxford University Press.
LÖFFLER, L. G.
1967   Symmetrische und Asymmetrische Allianzsysteme. *Bijdragen tot de Taal-, Land- en Volkenkunde*, **123**: 125-33.
LUCICH, P.
1968   *The Development of Omaha Kinship Terminologies in Three Australian Aboriginal Tribes of the Kimberley Division, Western Australia*. Canberra: Institute of Aboriginal Studies.

MANT, G.
1946   Letters Recount the Death of a Tribe (Dieri). *South-Western Pacific*, no. 11: 25-7.
MATHEWS, R. H.
1908   Marriage and Descent in the Aranda Tribe, Central Australia. *American Anthropologist*, **10**: 88-102.
MAUSS, M.
1920   L'extension du potlatch en Mélanésie. *Anthropologie*, **30**: 396-7.
MAYBURY-LEWIS, D.
1970   Science by Association. In Hayes and Hayes (eds.) 1970: 133-9.
MEISSEL, G.
1871   Lake Kopperamana Vocabulary. In Taplin 1871: 88.
MURDOCK, G. P.
1949   *Social Structure*. New York: Macmillan.
1960   (ed.) *Social Structure in Southeast Asia*. Viking Fund Publications in Anthropology, no. 29. Chicago: Quadrangle Books.
NADEL, S. F.
1937   Review of Bateson 1936. *Man*, **37**: 44-6.
NEEDHAM, R.
1958   The Formal Analysis of Prescriptive Patrilateral Cross-Cousin Marriage. *Southwestern Journal of Anthropology*, **14**: 199-219.
1960a   Patrilateral Prescriptive Alliance and the Ungarinyin. *Southwestern Journal of Anthropology*, **16**: 274-91.
1960b   Lineal Equations in a Two-section System. *Journal of the Polynesian Society*, **69**: 23-9.
1960c   A Structural Analysis of Aimol Society. *Bijdragen tot de Taal-, Land- en Volkenkunde*, **161**: 81-108.
1960d   Descent Systems and Ideal Language. *Philosophy of Science*, **27**: 96-101.

1961   Notes on the Analysis of Asymmetric Alliance. *Bijdragen tot de Taal-, Land- en Volkenkunde*, **117**: 93-117.

1962a   *Structure and Sentiment.* Chicago: University of Chicago Press.

1962b   Genealogy and Category in Wikmunkan Society. *Ethnology*, **1**: 223-63.

1962c   Notes on Comparative Method and Prescriptive Alliance. *Bijdragen tot de Taal-, Land- en Volkenkunde*, **118**: 160-82.

1963   A Synoptic Examination of Anāl Society. *Ethnos*, **29**: 219-36

1964a   Descent, Category, and Alliance in Sirionó Society. *Southwestern Journal of Anthropology*, **20**: 229-40.

1964b   The Mota Problem and its Lessons. *Journal of the Polynesian Society*, **73**: 302-14.

1964c   [On Group Marriage and Prescriptive Alliance.] In Lienhardt 1964: 125-7.

1966   Terminology and Alliance, I: Garo, Manggarai. *Sociologus*, **16**: 141-57.

1967a   Terminology and Alliance, II: Mapuche, Conclusions. *Sociologus*, **17**: 39-54.

1967b   Right and Left in Nyoro Symbolic Classification. *Africa*, **37**: 425-51.

1969   Gurage Social Classification: Formal Notes on an unusual System. *Africa*, **39**: 153-66.

1970   Endeh, II: Test and Confirmation. *Bijdragen tot de Taal-, Land- en Volkenkunde*, **126**: 246-58.

1971a   (ed.) *Rethinking Kinship and Marriage.* (ASA Monographs 11.) London: Tavistock Publications.

1971b   Remarks on the Analysis of Kinship and Marriage. In Needham (ed.) 1971a: 1-34.

PALMER, E.
1884   Notes on Some Australian Tribes. *Journal of the Anthropological Institute*, **13**: 335-46.

PIAGET, J.
1968   *Le Structuralisme.* Paris: Presses Universitaires de France.

PINK, O.
1936   The Landowners in the Northern Division of the Aranda Tribe, Central Australia. *Oceania*, **6**: 275-305.

PLANERT, W.
1908   Australische Forschungen, II: Dieri-Grammatik. *Zeitschrift für Ethnologie*, **40**: 691.

POWDERMAKER, H.
1940   Review of Bateson 1936. *American Anthropologist*, **42**: 162-4.

[RADCLIFFE-] BROWN, A. R.
1914   The Relationship System of the Dieri. *Man*, **14**: 53-6.

RADCLIFFE-BROWN, A. R.
1931   *The Social Organization of Australian Tribes*. Melbourne:
            Macmillan.
1951   Murngin Social Organization. *American Anthropologist*,
            53: 37-55.

REVEL, J. F.
1957   *Pourquoi des philosophes*. Paris: Pauvert.

RIVERS, W. H. R.
1912   The Sociological Significance of Myth. *Folk-lore*, **23**:
            307-31.
1968   *Kinship and Social Organization*. London: Athlone Press.

RIVIÈRE, P. G.
1971   Marriage: a reassessment. In Needham (ed.) 1971a: 57-74.

SCHNEIDER, D. M.
1965   Some Muddles in the Models. In *The Relevance of Models
            in Social Anthropology*. (ASA Monographs 1.) London:
            Tavistock Publications.

SCHOLTE, B.
1970   Epistemic Paradigms: Some Problems in Cross-cultural
            Research on Social Anthropological History and Theory.
            In Hayes and Hayes (eds.) 1970: 108-22.

SHARP, B.
1935   Semi-Moieties in North-Western Queensland. *Oceania*,
            6: 158-69.

SIEBERT, O.
1910   Sagen und Sitten der Dieri und Nachbarstämme in
            Zentral-Australien. *Globus*, **97**: 44-50; 53-9.

SIMONIS, Y.
1968   *Claude Lévi-Strauss ou la 'Passion de l'inceste': Introduction
            au structuralisme*. Paris: Aubier-Montaigne.

SPENCER B.
1914   *Native Tribes of the Northern Territory of Australia*.
            London: Macmillan.

SPENCER, B., and GILLEN, F. J.
1899   *The Native Tribes of Central Australia*. London: Macmillan.
1904   *The Northern Tribes of Central Australia*. London: Mac-
            millan.
1927   *The Arunta*. London: Macmillan.

SPERBER, D.
1968   Le structuralisme en anthropologie. In Ducrot *et al.* 1968.
            169-238.

STREHLOW, C.
1907-20   *Die Aranda- und Loritja-Stämme in Zentral-Australien.*
           5 parts. Frankfurt-am-Main: Joseph Baer.

STREHLOW, T. G. H.
1947   *Aranda Traditions.* Melbourne: Melbourne University
           Press.

TAPLIN, G.
1871   Notes on a Table of Australian Languages. *Journal of the
           Anthropological Institute,* **1**: 84-8.

THOMAS, N. W.
1906a   Dr Howitt's Defense of Group-marriage. *Folk-lore,* **17**:
           294-307.
1906b   *Kinship Organisations and Group Marriage in Australia.*
           Cambridge: Cambridge University Press.
1907   Australian Marriage Customs. *Folk-lore,* **18**: 306-18.

TINDALE, N. B.
1940   Distribution of Australian Aboriginal Tribes. *Transactions
           of the Royal Society of South Australia,* **64**: 140-231.

WARNER, L. W.
1933   Kinship Morphology of Forty-one North Australian
           Tribes. *American Anthropologist,* **35**: 63-86.

WEIL, A.
1949   Sur l'étude algébraique de certains types de lois de mariage
           (système Murngin). Appendix to the first part of Lévi-
           Strauss 1949: 278-85.

WHITE, H. C.
1963   *An Anatomy of Kinship.* Englewood Cliffs, N. J.: Prentice-
           Hall.

WHITE, L.
1948   The Definition and Prohibition of Incest. *American
           Anthropologist,* **61**: 1042-59.

WOODS, J. D.
1879   *The Native Tribes of South Australia.* Adelaide.

Name Index

Bateson, G., xv, 80, 81, 82, 83, 84, 85, 86, 87, 88, 89, 90, 91, 93, 96, 98, 99, 101, 102, 103, 104, 106, 107, 108, 150
Berndt, R. M., 41, 72, 146, 149, 150
Berndt, R. M. & C. Berndt, 42, 150
Berndt, R. M. & T. Vogelsang, 149, 150
Boudon, R., 1, 17, 18, 20, 35, 150
Brough-Smyth, R., 150
Brüggemann, W., 82n
Bush, R., 17, 18, 124, 126, 132, 133, 135, 151

Cornblit, O., xiii
Courrège, Ph., 124, 129, 130, 131, 132, 133, 151
Craig, B., 40n

Darwin, Charles, 49
Douglas, M., 7, 151
Ducrot, O. *et al.*, 151, 158
Dumont, L., 69n, 107, 111, 122, 123, 151
Durkheim, E., 2-3, 9, 26, 32, 33, 34, 49, 71, 76, 111, 151

Elkin, A. P., 40, 41, 43n, 44, 45, 55-9, 61, 65, 66, 67, 71, 72, 75, 81n, 146, 151
Ellis, Havelock, 9

Fison, L., 5, 51, 52, 134, 151
Fison, L. & A. W. Howitt, 54, 152
Flierl, 72, 148
Forge, A., 81n, 152
Fox, R., 18, 19, 152
Frazer, J. G., 9, 41, 44, 54, 152
Fry, H. K., 30, 78-9n, 152

Gason, S., 27, 40, 41, 42, 44, 50, 59, 72, 146, 147, 152
Gatti, G., 42, 70n, 152
Grant, P., xiii
Greenway, J., 40n, 78n, 152
Guilbaud, G. Th., 124

Hayes, E. N. & T. Hayes, 152, 156, 158
Helms, 43
Hocart, A. M., 3, 7, 108, 153
Hodson, T. C., 5, 133n, 153
Howitt, A. W., 5, 27, 40, 41, 42, 43, 44, 45, 46, 47, 48, 49, 50, 51, 52, 54, 55, 58, 59, 70, 72, 146, 147, 148, 153
Howitt, A. W. & O. Siebert, 43, 153

Subject Index

adoption, Iatmül, 87
Aimol, 109
alliance, 4, 80, 121
  asymmetric, 48, 97, 107
  Iatmül, 80, 81, 96, 112, 141;
    see also Iatmül, alliance
  Kachin, 97n
  prescriptive, 100; *see also* pre-
    scriptive systems
  see also marriage
alternate generations, 111, 112,
  141; *see also* Mara
Arabana, descent among, 27
Aranda, 126, 127, 130, 131, 141,
  143
  descent among, 25-6, 27, 28, 30,
    33, 109, 112
  Dieri system and, 39, 54, 55,
    58, 59, 60, 63, 64, 66, 74,
    109
  exchange among, 25
    of sisters, 25
  Mara and, 112-13, 119
  marriage among, 28, 112-13
  moieties among, 26, 27, 28, 30-1,
    32, 33n, 34, 109, 122,
    134
  Northern, 25, 28
  residence among, 25, 26, 34
  Southern, 25, 27, 28

subsections among, 25, 26, 28,
  111
terminology, kinship, 29, 30, 32,
  64, 66, 74, 97, 111, 112,
  116, 119, 121, 122, 123
totemic system of, 27, 31, 32,
  33
Aranta, 113
Arunta, 113, 129
  descent among, 27
Asia, South East, classification in,
  100
Australian systems, 22, 52, 56,
  97n
  see also Arabana, Aranda,
    Aranta, Arunta, Dieri,
    Jantruwanta, Jauraworka,
    Kamilaroi, Kariera,
    Laierdila, Mara,
    Murngin, Ngameni,
    Warrai, Warramunga,
    Wikmunkan

betrothal
  among Dieri, 56-7, 73
  among Itamül, 108
  among Mara, 116
bride-price/-wealth; *see* marriage,
  payments

categories, social, 3
Chin, 109
choice, 37
classification, social, 5, 48, 68, 98,
    100, 108, 122
consanguinity, 3-4
cousin(s); *see* cross-cousins and
    parallel-cousins
cross-cousins, 15
    marriage of
        bilateral, 35
        matrilateral, 22-3, 35
        patrilateral, 23, 35
Crow Indians, 19
'Crow–Omaha' systems, 19, 20;
    see also terminology, kin-
    ship

descent, 111
    Arabana, 27
    Aranda, 25, 26, 27, 28, 30, 33,
        109
    Arunta, 27
    Dieri, 42, 44, 48, 61-3, 71,
        78-9n
    'double', 55, 61-3, 122
    Iatmül, 83, 91, 92
    in Lévi-Strauss, 23-4, 26, 33
    Mara, 115
Dieri, 112
    Aranda system and, 39, 54, 55,
        58, 59, 60, 63, 64, 66, 74,
        109
    betrothal among, 56-7, 73
    descent among, 42, 44, 48, 61-3,
        71, 78-9n
    disintegration of, 41
    early accounts of, 27, 40-1
    genealogical levels among, 47-8,
        68, 72-3, 96
    inheritance among, 42, 44, 70
    initiation among, 59
    interpretations of,
        Elkin, 55-8, 66-7, 71-2, 146

Howitt, 48-52, 146, 147
Lane and Lane, 61-3
Lang, 49, 50
Lévi-Strauss, 39, 40, 59-61,
    63-6, 74-5, 77-8, 141, 143
Radcliffe-Brown, 39, 52-5, 58
Thomas, 49, 50-1
location of, 41-2
marriage among, 39, 44, 47,
    50-1, 54, 58, 63, 70, 73, 76,
    118
moiety system, 39, 42-5, 48,
    58-9, 62-3, 77-8, 109, 111,
    134
myths among, 42, 43, 59
procreation concepts among,
    58-9
residence among, 40, 42, 122
sister-exchange among, 45, 47
terminology, kinship, 45-8,
    48-52, 53, 54-5, 56-7,
    59-61, 62, 63-9, 70-5, 78,
    97, 109, 111, 116, 121,
    122, 123, 138, 146-9
totemic system, 42, 43, 44-5
    49, 55, 59, 76-7
divorce, 89, 100, 104, 108
dual organization, 22
Dutch anthropology; *see* Leiden
    School of

endogamy, 90
evolutionary theories, 49, 111
    Morgan and, 44, 48
exchange, 4-5, 21-4
    continuous, 22-3
    discontinuous, 23
    generalized, 21-4, 39, 76, 78
        109, 141
    marriage as, 4, 13; *see als*
        marriage *and* alliance
    of prestations, 100-3, 108
    restricted, 21-2, 24, 25, 34, 3.
        39, 76, 78, 109, 141